the

complete

Notes

from

the

Universe

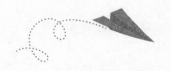

NEW PERSPECTIVES FROM
AN OLD FRIEND

the

complete

Notes

from

the

Universe

THE BESTSELLING TRILOGY NOW
ROLLED INTO ONE VOLUME

MIKE DOOLEY

New York Times bestselling author

ATRIA PAPERBACK
New York London Toronto Sydney New Delhi

BEYOND WORDS
Hillsboro, Oregon

ATRIA PAPERBACK
An Imprint of Simon & Schuster, Inc.
1230 Avenue of the Americas
New York, NY 10020
www.beyondword.com

BEYOND WORDS
1750 S.W. Skyline Blvd., Suite 20
Portland, Oregon 97221-2543
503-531-8700 / 503-531-8773 fax

Compilation of text previously published under the titles:
Notes from the Universe © 2003, 2007 (978-1-58270-176-9)
More Notes from the Universe © 2005, 2008 (978-1-58270-184-4)
Even More Notes from the Universe © 2005, 2008 (978-1-58270-186-8)

Managing Editor: Lindsay S. Easterbrooks-Brown
Editor: Emmalisa Sparrow Wood
Proofreader: Madison Schultz
Design: Devon Smith
Composition: William H. Brunson Typography Services

First Beyond Words/Atria paperback edition September 2020

Manufactured in the United States of America

10 9 8 7 6 5 4 3 2 1

Library of Congress Cataloging-in-Publication Data

Names: Dooley, Mike, 1961- author.
Title: The complete notes from the universe : new perspectives from an old
  friend / Mike Dooley.
Description: New York : Atria Paperback ; Hillsboro, Oregon : Beyond Words,
  2020. | Summary: "For the first time ever, the hugely popular Notes from
  the Universe trilogy is being offered as one large volume, making it
  even easier to share the love and wisdom of Mike Dooley's Universe.
  The Complete Notes from the Universe is a collection
  of over 600 Notes (including 55 that have never before been published), with
  a new foreword and introduction. Prepare to fall in love with your life,
  all over again"-- Provided by publisher.
Identifiers: LCCN 2020005189 (print) | LCCN 2020005190 (ebook) | ISBN
  9781582707297 (paperback) | ISBN 9781982145668 (ebook)
Subjects: LCSH: Life--Miscellanea. | Wisdom--Miscellanea. |
  Spirituality--Miscellanea. | Occultism--Miscellanea.
Classification: LCC BF1999 .D61525 2020 (print) | LCC BF1999 (ebook) |
  DDC 158--dc23
LC record available at https://lccn.loc.gov/2020005189
LC ebook record available at https://lccn.loc.gov/2020005190

The corporate mission of Beyond Words Publishing, Inc.: *Inspire to Integrity*

To the brightest stars—
brother, sister, daughter, wife—
in my universe.

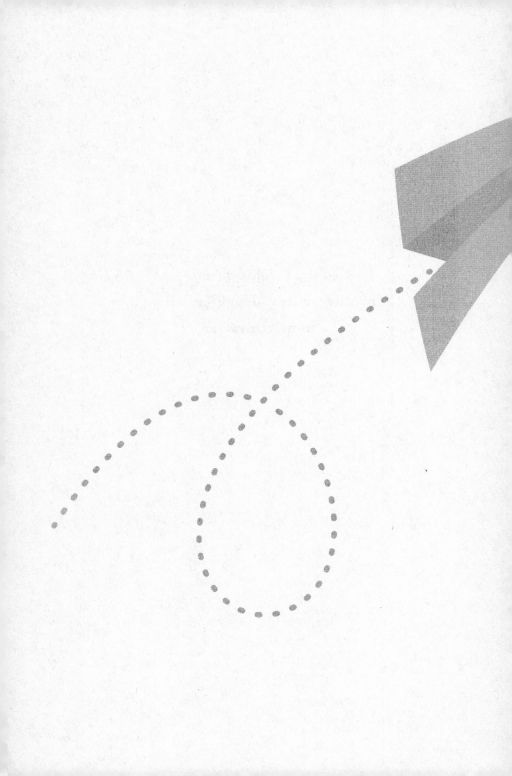

If I told you there've been no mistakes,

that I understand every decision you've ever made, and that the challenges you've faced, you've faced for everyone, would you listen?

If I told you that what you dream of, I dream of for you, that the only things "meant to be" are what you decide upon, and that all that stands between you and the life of your dreams are the thoughts you choose to think, would you try to understand?

And if I told you that you are never alone, that there are angels who sing your name in praise, and that I couldn't possibly be any more proud of you than I already am, would you believe me?

Would you? Even if I pulled your leg, made you blush, and winked between my lines?

Then I shall . . .

FOREWORD
by Leon Logothetis

About ten years ago, a friend told me about Notes from the Universe, sent to subscribers by email, and while I don't remember the first one I received, I will never forget when the following email arrived in my inbox:

Everyone's scared, Leon.
Few carry on.

Keep calm,
The Universe

PS—I mean *really* carry on, Leon,
as if it were your reason for being.

I printed it out, and no matter where I was in the world—no matter the adventure—I always carried that personalized Note from the Universe with me, and it eventually became a bookmark for whatever book I was reading at the time.

I later remember filming season one of my Netflix series *The Kindness Diaries* and hitting a rather rough spot in Vietnam. My bike was impounded (which, no surprise, wasn't a good thing), and I had nowhere to stay. It looked like the entire adventure was coming to an inglorious end. To take a break from the madness, I found a quiet place to read, attempting to calm myself down. When I opened my book, my Note bookmarker popped out and I knew immediately—on the deepest level—that everything was going to be okay. And it was.

I still get the Notes by email and have been amazed by how often they have said exactly what I most needed to hear. They are a wonderful guiding light, offering reminders of faith in this sometimes paradoxical world. I spend much of my days traveling and filming shows, and often it doesn't always go according to plan, but I have learned that Sir Winston Churchill was right when he said "Never give in. Never give in, never, never, never, never—in nothing, great or small..."

We all know that the quality of our thoughts directly impacts the quality of everything else in our world. This is how the Notes have made a life-changing difference for me. They remind me that I'm part of something bigger—much bigger—and that our dreams really can come true. They've also shown me that if I have faith in the end result, the path there doesn't feel as precarious (and I have been on some precarious paths).

Mike Dooley's Notes have also validated the most important elements of my own evolving wisdom (if I can claim as much):

- ✓ We are all adored.
- ✓ Kindness is a superpower.
- ✓ Love is the greatest thing we can give or receive.
- ✓ Setbacks are actually calculated setups for greatness.
- ✓ And *everything* is possible!

Over the last few years, the Notes have added to the joy and meaning of my life. It's my wish that they do the same for you.

May you find in this beautiful compilation inspiration to follow your dreams and the power to carry on, as you learn to create the life you were born to live.

Love, Leon

INTRODUCTION

I used to have a recurring dream experience in which, mid-dream, I'd begin to excitedly wonder: Is this a dream? *I think this is a dream! Am I really dreaming? Whoa! If I'm really dreaming, I could do absolutely anything!*

How cool would that be, to wake up *inside* of a dream? But the same two issues always arose:

1. I simply could not think of *what to do* if it was a dream.
2. I'd find my surroundings to be so *exactly* like those of time and space—the sites, sounds, and details were so complete, intricate, and unexpected (as I gazed down a random road, into the sky, or at my feet)—I concluded it simply *could not* be a dream.

I'd then drift back into deep sleep.

What would you do, mid-dream, if you found out you were dreaming? And how would you determine whether or not it really was a dream?

Hours later, I'd awaken to my alarm clock and recall the dream, happy to realize I *had indeed* awoken within it but deeply disappointed for not gaining any traction.

I wondered for decades why I'd sometimes have these experiences until it dawned on me that they were the perfect metaphor for *the dream of life*. And with that realization, they stopped.

I'm hardly alone thinking that we're all dreaming right now. Einstein said, "Reality is merely an illusion, albeit a very persistent one." Yet we're all so enthralled by *our* illusions and the drama of our lives played out among them, we rarely, if ever, consider them anything less than "reality." Moreover, when some of us briefly find ourselves "half awake," momentarily claiming to know that life is but a dream, we hardly know what to do with ourselves!

Take right now, for example: You sense this is true—your life *is* a dream. You know that matter isn't solid, but whirling, organized energy. Yet in spite of this awareness, instead of seizing on it, you'll soon arise from your chair, maybe make some coffee, check your cell phone, and drift back into "deep sleep"—which is to say, you'll no longer realize you're dreaming. And what would you do anyway, if you carried this dream realization with you into the world beyond your chair? Aimlessly look for proof? Doubt yourself? And *then* drift back into deep sleep? Exactly the dream experience I used to have.

I believe this paradox *is* the hook of time and space spoken of in the Bible, the Bhagavad Gita, other holy books, and mentioned by countless teachers *and students* of reality. Conceptually, it's not hard to miss: the idea that time and space form *baseline reality*—and that where we come from and will go to counts less—is preposterous. It's the proof of this that defies all logic, because we typically look for evidence that we are dreaming within the illusions; within the dream itself!

The Garden of Eden was *and is* a similar metaphor for life on earth. A blissful, illusionary oasis of divine creation (*our own creation*, we being immortal aspects of Divine Intelligence "made in 'His' likeness"). Yet biting into the apple signified our choosing to believe *and act* within the dream as if *the illusions (the apple) were, in fact, real,* instead of our own "holographic" projection. From that fateful moment, the original sin being committed, we "fell" from grace, or from fully knowing that we did *and still do* have dominion over the paradise we had created in the greatest dream of all.

Actually, it's a sad but understandable misrepresentation to say we "fell" when, clearly, we're still exactly where we began—within a paradise we've fashioned in the mind of God. But it was diabolical to imply, as religions have done, that we were no longer living in "grace." *As if* the dreamer(s) had not intended to be drawn into, and be spellbound by, the beauty of such a paradise and was/were not still in control, playing their unknown dream out in the "palm of God's own hand"—safe, eternal, and still all-powerful.

Denying knowledge of our matter-streaming-selves, we end up contending with the stuff of our dreams instead of shaping them, seeing ourselves as a victim of circumstances rather than their creator—even as we shape and create them. By creating unknowingly, we deny ourselves leverage to change those apparitions (manifestations) that displease. Worse, by frowning upon and focusing on whatever we find unpleasant, we perpetuate its existence in our dreams!

I've been "half awake" since I turned twenty years old—which adds up to almost forty years now—very slowly waking up, ever more mindful, year after year, that I'm dreaming, practicing always to remember at all times life's secret hook, determined to live my dream life happily through:

1. Understanding its few and simple absolutes (we're One, love is all, thoughts become things),
2. Introspection,
3. Creative visualization, and
4. Taking action.

These steps, I've read (and found), are how to shape the dream of life from within it, *even before you fully awaken*. And that's one of the freakiest of things. You don't have to be fully "self-realized" within the dream (by consciously knowing you're dreaming), to *kind-of* get that you are, to be aware enough to know that your thoughts today will shape your circumstances tomorrow, and to start making your dreams come true!

This is the basis for the idea that "positive thinking" is worthwhile and that creative visualization has merit. *Our* dreams are made up of *our* thoughts. Change your thoughts and you will change your dream/ life. You will bring about what you think about. Even if you don't know that you will. *Even if you don't know you're dreaming!*

What a ride these almost forty years have been! By virtually every inner and outer measure, I've accomplished all I've ever set out to do. Not to say I haven't had my share of pains, spills, and seeming disasters. My proverbial dark night of the soul came at thirty-nine years of age. My business was liquidated, my finances were a train wreck, and I'd just discovered my girlfriend had a boyfriend (and it wasn't me).

I wanted to die but figured that would suck even more. So I drilled down to truth and told myself, "While you may not know how you created this mess, you damn sure know how to change it! *You're dreaming, Dooley!* You're f'ing *dreaming!* So in spite of appearances, it's time to start dreaming new dreams, thinking new thoughts, speaking new words, showing up with new baby steps, and for good measure . . . it wouldn't hurt if you prayed on your knees to God every night before you go to sleep." Really. I was raised a Catholic, and I was desperate.

I can tell you about this now, given how fantastic it all turned out, but back then, it was embarrassing to be me. I was grateful then, however, to hide most of my pain and praying from the world as I got busy "knocking on doors and turning over stones," doing all I could with all I had from where I was, which included dreaming big dreams and physically showing up for them.

One of those small steps was sending out emailed inspiration that was supposed to help snap readers out of their spiritual slumber into the truth of life's beauty and their own power—*exactly the kind of emails I wanted to be receiving.* Actually, these were never too popular; probably owing to them being sent by some guy subscribers never met and didn't know. But those emails paved the way for Notes from the Universe, which have given me a fairytale life.

Today, I'm still as much a student as I am a teacher. But in the past twenty years, I've written seventeen books, traveled extensively to the coolest and farthest corners of the globe (blissfully teaching what I've learned), got married, finally became a dad, and feel blessed beyond what I could have earlier conceived of as possible. Essentially, my success has stemmed from my own waking up to the fact that I'm dreaming. And in doing so, my life has shifted from battling the world around me to first crafting within my mind.

The praying on my knees absolutely helped too, not because it "activated" God (who's already working 24/7/365 on all our behalves), but because it helped me to define and focus on what I wanted and helped me to believe that I wasn't just mere-mortal Mike, alone in the cold hard world, but that I was supported, as if magically, by a loving Divine Intelligence.

One of the coolest, happiest things of my life today (other than being a husband and a dad) is sharing what I've learned in any way I can, from the first Notes sent by email to the book you now hold in your hands. This trilogy is composed of the earliest Notes ever written—some are a bit offbeat (that's how I wrote back then!) and others were tweaked for clarity—still, they've almost made me famous, paving the way for thousands more to be written and ultimately living a life I love. As a bonus, this book also includes more than fifty personal favorites that have never before been published. All of which have helped me wake up, and they may help you wake up too.

Dear reader, *you're dreaming right now,*
and you can do absolutely anything you want . . .

How You Might Use This Book

When these Notes were first sent out by email to subscribers, the most common reply I received (and still receive) was that more often than not, day after day, readers were amazed by the uncanny timing of each Note as it related to exactly where they were in their respective lives. "How could you know? Even my closest friends don't have a clue!" or "I was eating French toast at 4 AM when today's Note arrived . . . and I had to call and wake my mother to share that the PS asked, 'More syrup?' just as I was reaching for it!" or "As I was worrying about the sad ending of my marriage and its potential effect on my children, tears and tissues everywhere, today's Note arrived telling me 'If you only knew just how incredibly well everything is going to turn out, for you and those close to you, right now you'd likely feel light as a feather, free as the wind, happy, confident, giddy . . .'"

How, indeed? The obvious answer is that while 800,000 people receive the exact same Note, none of them interprets it the same way. Each reader filters it through his or her own thoughts and circumstances. The not-so-obvious answer is that in these hallowed jungles of time and space, things are not as they appear. We've been told since our lives began that we are but mere bystanders to the glory of life and that everything happens along a rigid, linear time line. The truth, however, is that we're each the co-creator of all that we share, and our experiences spring from an eternal now. It's only our exclusive reliance upon our physical senses to interpret life that makes this so challenging to grasp. And so, just as those who witness a beautiful sunrise actually participate in its co-creation, so too in some mystical, magical way are the readers of these words and the daily Notes their co-creators—whether they were received as an email in the "past" or randomly chosen from the pages now before you.

Go on. Give it a try. Just open this book to any "random" page and see what's waiting for you! You're really quite the writer, you know.

the

complete

Notes

from

the

Universe

To clarify "eternal"

just a smidge...

Once the river of time has rounded her final bend, and the last
star in the sky has brightened its last night, and every child who
may ever be conceived has been given ten thousand names...
we will have just begun.

Got time?

When I think of how much you and I have
to look forward to, I almost get dizzy with joy.

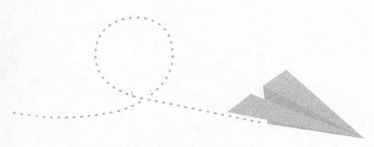

It never fails to amaze me.

Create a paradise out of the ether. Throw in some wildlife,
volcanoes, and windstorms. Some iguanas, koalas, and waterfalls.
Come back a few billion years later, and just when it looks like
the whole place is going to implode—with pollution, disease, and
war; famine, fatigue, and fright—there are still those who see the
beauty. Who act with kindness. And who live
with hope and gratitude.

Actually, they carry the entire planet.

Who'd have thunk?

Yeah, okay. Guilty.

Want to know what's better

than having it all? Way, way better?

Not having it all, but knowing of its inevitability, in a never-ending adventure that's just barely begun.

Yeeeeeehaaaaaaaaaaaaaaaa!

Kind of like Friday just before the weekend.

How to make anything happen . . .

Act as if it already has, and never look back.

I should have shared this earlier,

but, well, I'm the Universe and I've been busy.

In the beginning, long before there were even beaches to walk along, clouds to float upon, or stars to wish on, I dreamed of you and your happiness.

And everything that has ever been added since was to that end.

See? You are so much more to me than just pretty planet decoration.

Hmmm!

I'm doing a little paperwork, and I have a quota system here for doling out wealth, abundance, friends, love, laughter . . . you name it. Says here you signed up for "it all," but I've hardly given you your share.

Tell me . . . Are you coming to me for these things?
Leveraging my love and engaging the magic?

Or are you trying to muster them up on your own . . . ?

Of course you're strong enough.
Or what would be the point?

Go forth,
The Universe

And rock the world.

The very most
anyone ever has to overcome is today.

Which is actually the "height limit" on all metaphorical lions,
tigers, and bears.

Double G-R-R-R-R...
The Universe

PS—Not that any given day isn't also the very most anyone could
ever hope to receive

Ain't it grand?

Doesn't it boggle your mind?
The harmony, the splendor, the beauty.
The intricacies, the synchronicities, the staggering perfection.

Do you ever wonder how it all came about?
Do you think I studied quarks, atoms, and molecules?
That I drew schematics for the sun, the moon, and the stars;
the otter, the Gila monster, and the penguin?
Do you think I painted every zebra, flower, and butterfly?

Or, do you think, I simply imagined the end result?

And that's all you ever have to do.

I hated school.

Do you think

you're going to feel cheated on the day you discover that your
countless successes were pretty much inevitable? And that all the
doubts, the fretting, and the worries were a silly waste of time?

Or do you think you'll just roll with
things . . . carefree . . . blissful . . . and with a permanent
catlike smile on your face?

Yeah. Roll, and the other stuff.
That's what we said you'd do.

So . . . how about it?

The Universe
(and all her proud felines)

Do you know
what "unlimited" means?

It means you decide—*everything*.

The most fun
a baby soul can have comes from watching.

The most fun a young soul can have comes from doing.

And the most fun an old soul can have doesn't
come from anything.

Crazy like a fox,
The Universe

PS—Not that old souls aren't often the first to the playground,
dance floor, or hoedown, but that they can also have fun
anywhere, anytime, like right here and now.

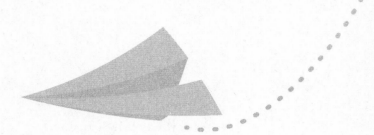

To set the record straight:

However cool you think it might be to have an out-of-body
experience—floating over your house, flying through space,
traversing the past, present, and future—let me tell you, it'll never
be as cool as being in the one you have now. Walking barefoot
in the grass, floating in a sun-drenched pool,
and dancing alone in the dark.

You so "fly,"
The Universe

*Trust me, from here, getting into-body
is considered the most sacred of all sacreds.*

Whoops... I did it again.

Took a little nap, had a few dreams, and worlds were born.
Planets spun and cooled. Continents rose and fell.
And civilizations clashed and united.

Actually, it's quite good fun. But I also dreamed I was you. And
in that dream, for a spell, I didn't remember
I was also the Universe.

It was frightful, actually. Just about scared me to death until,
as you, I slowly remembered who I was. And in those waking
moments, it was as if the earth shook, the seas danced, and the
skies rejoiced almost as much as myself. As if they were waking up,
too. It was the most beautiful, sublime, intoxicating rush of
pure joy I think I've ever known.

How I wish I could tell you more. But like a farmer eager for the
new crop, any rush to harvest would spoil the yield.
Besides, words would utterly fail me.

By the simple act of thinking,

vortexes are created, invisible energies are applied, and circumstances begin creeping to make real what was previously just imagined. This supernatural pull of your thoughts continues long after you think them, whenever there follows intent, expectation, and action; moving mountains, parting rivers, and doing the "impossible" until there is the inevitable manifestation.

This is how your "thoughts become things."
How they physically become things in a dimension that already exists, with billions of players and massive momentum. Not by appearing out of thin air, but through a manipulation of forces in the unseen that literally begin shifting, morphing, and rearranging all of the elements in your life so as to deliver to you the nearest equivalent of what you've been thinking.

In other words, the "law of attraction."

"Thoughts become things" explains the law of attraction. It's why there is a law of attraction. And unlike any other three words in all the vocabularies of all the languages in all the world, "thoughts become things" tells you exactly where you fit into the picture, as the thinker, the decision maker over what you will think about, revealing your power as a supernatural, all-powerful, unlimited CREATOR.

But, of course, many prefer not to think of themselves as so phenomenally powerful.

Okay, for just five minutes

forget the bucks. Forget your soul mate, too.
Forget the new car, the "home run," and being on *Oprah*.
Forget your fears, your problems, and your pain. And during
those five minutes, feel the feelings you most want to feel,
for the rest of your life.

It might seem awkward, that's okay.
It might seem silly, too. And I can just about guarantee, at first,
it'll feel utterly futile . . . until your entire life begins to change.

If I were a beggar, I'd beg you. If I prayed in question marks,
this is what I'd ask for. And if I could implore you to do anything,
let this be it. Because nothing else that you might ever do will
have as profound an effect on your fortunes, friendships, and
happiness; in navigating the illusions, manifesting what you
want, and avoiding what you dread; as this little five-minute drill
performed just once a day, on as many days as you
remember to do it.

And just so you know, if you do this right now or even every day
for the rest of your life, I'll add back those five minutes to
each of the days you do it. I'll just sneak 'em in there,
and they'll feel like ten.

But . . . not a word to anyone.

And that reminds me,

since I don't pray in question marks, I hope you don't, either.

You know, "Can I, please...? Will you, please...? If I do X, or sacrifice Y, will you do Z...?" We have "spam filters" here, too, and since only you can answer those questions, they kind of just go in one port and out the other.

Now, if you pray in "thank-yous", especially for stuff you haven't yet received or experienced (but as if you already had), those we all hear.

Amen!
The Universe

It takes a really special person,

someone quite extraordinary, to find true happiness in the lap of luxury surrounded by wealth and abundance, friends and laughter, and choices, choices, choices.

And funnily enough, it's usually the exact same kind of person who can be happy without all that, spending time alone, maybe with a book, or some tools, or a dog for the odd distraction.

Get my drift?

Just do what you can

with what's before you today . . . and leave "spectacular" to me.

'Kay?

*The same goes for "profound," "stellar,"
"revolutionary," and "outrageous."*

Jambo*! Universe here...

Golly, do I ever need a vacation.

Can you imagine having the entire world spin in the palm of your hand? Writing the script to history? Being able to change the course of eternity by just changing your mind? Kind of far-out, isn't it? But it's all right here in the brochure. Read it myself,

"Spellbinding! Intoxicating! The ultimate escape! Join billions on an unforgettable adventure into the jungles of Time and Space, to a paradise found where you are master of your destiny, all things are possible, and your every thought changes everything. So real, you may even forget who you are!"

Perfect for me, bags are packed.

Be cool (just brushing up on the lingo),
The Universe

PS—Let's do lunch.

*Jambo! (Swahili for "hello"; Adventurese for "I'm glad our paths have crossed...")

"Grasshopper,"

you may not always know what your invisible, limiting beliefs are.

But you do always know the kinds of empowering beliefs you'd like to possess. And so, one decision at a time, one day at a time, you can choose to behave accordingly. And thereby effectively kick some wicked, limiting-belief butt.

For every decision, crossroad, or act of faith,
choose with the mind of the highest within you.
Until that's all there is.

For every fork in the road,

there are often two paths from which to choose . . . the one you "should" take and the one you want to take.

Take the second.
Always take the second.
I did.

Could life rock any more than it does?

There hasn't been one

single day of your life when the world hasn't been made a better place by your presence in it.

If you only knew.

Next time you feel really hurt,

really angry, or really, really upset, and you're sure that even I
have been violated, shaken, and humbled, quick, check and see
if the sky is any less blue, the sun any less radiant, the birds have
stopped singing, or the flowers have lost their scent.

I'll wager you'll find that life has gone on much as before.
Too consumed by the powers of now and the inevitabilities of
love, understanding, and eternal life to have even missed a beat.

Oh-wee-oh,
The Universe

That's if there even is a next time.

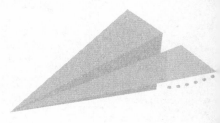

When you tough it out,

hold the line, and stay the course, I promise you there will soon
come a day when you look back over your shoulder, shake your
head in dismay, and seriously wonder what all the fuss was about.

Just like all the other times.

In fact, in not so many days from today, it will become clear as a
bell that you did have enough time, that you were never alone,
and that all of us in the unseen were working double time
to help make possible "the time of your life."

Yeeeeeehaaaaaaaaaaaaaaa! XOXOXO.

There's *always* another way.
Always.

Has it occurred to you

that wherever you go, you are my eyes, my ears, and my voice;
my arms, my legs, and my everything else, too?

Well, I vote for more flowers, more music, and more "I love
yous". More hugging, more skipping, and more naps.
But that's just me.

XXXXXXXXXXOOOOOOOOOOOO!

It was such a sad, sad picture.

She cried and cried, and ever so faintly murmured, "Oh, how I wish you were here with me now . . . That you could have always been with me . . . That we could have lived forever."

And so I whispered into her ear so softly that my words could only be felt, not heard, "He is, he will be, and you do."

She'll see.

Never trust appearances.

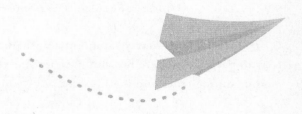

Phew . . . I need a break!

Tell you what, why don't you write your own Note today? To me?

You could say something like:

Jambo Universe, it's me!
Right, the good-looking, talented, sexy one for whom
the sun rises every day.

Anyway, just wanted to tell you that this adventure in time and
space has been awesome. Everything I ever expected it would
be. (Huh, imagine that.) It's been exactly as hard and as easy,
as challenging and as rewarding, as I've been telling myself.
(Hey, what a coincidence.)

And even though I know we are ONE, I still like thinking of you
"out there" somewhere, watching, loving, and protecting me.
(Hmm, could this also be why I sometimes feel alone?)

At any rate, I'm learning tons, having some fun, and really
looking forward to coming home one day.
(Unless, of course, I'm home now.)

Hey, since I have your attention, thanks for another
day in paradise. Where my thoughts become things, dreams never
stop coming true, and it all just keeps getting better and better.

You never cease to amaze me.

I hope you're loving your life.

And I do mean really, *really* loving your life.

Because right now there are so many others who are (loving your life). In time and space, and in the unseen.

No, not all of them will admit it, but I know these things, and one day you'll know them, too.

If you know what you want,

and you can remember that "thoughts become things"
is the only absolute law at play in time and space,
what else matters but what you choose to think today?

Cowabunga!

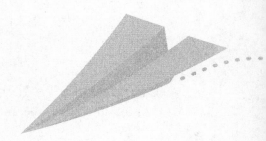

Can you hear it?

The entire Kingdom now beckons.

There are no tests, no hoops, and no limits.

All I have, I press to you at this very moment.

This is all you have to know.

And all you have to do is make room for the torrent that
will flow in direct proportion to your every preparation,
including what you do today.

You mean the world to me.

You know, a kind word

can move mountains and change lives.

But for those times when they've escaped you, when the right
thing wasn't said, and the time wasn't right to say it, kind thoughts
can do the same. And better, thoughts have a way of lingering,
seeking, and finding their intended beneficiary, unfettered
by time and space. So it's never too late to think 'em,
nor are you ever too far away.

Just a little something a tree once told me.

Guess who's thinking of you, right now?

You know that feeling,

when all of a sudden it seems like everything you ever wanted to happen starts happening at once. And you're totally blown away, on top of the world, almost feeling like you don't even have any more dreams because they're all coming true. Yet you're slammed because you're stretching yourself like you've never stretched before, just trying to keep up with them.

And every day some new magical realization hits you. And you've never felt so happy in your life. Except that you wish so badly that everyone close to you could have the same overwhelming experiences, the same sensory overload. And more, you wish everyone on the planet could feel it, too, at least just a little, because it's so intoxicating. And you feel like you now understand all the tough times, and all the slow days, and all the phases when it seemed like absolutely nothing was happening in your life.

And you wonder why you haven't always felt like this because what you feel is so much more than just the joy of dreams coming true. It's like you're feeling the heartbeat of everyone's life at once. And you realize there's always been so much more to be happy about than sad. And you wonder what it was that used to trouble you, and how it could have seemed so real, or how it could've seemed bigger than the beauty you now face. And you just shake your head, knowing how perfect everything is, how perfect it's always been, and how perfect it will always be. And you give thanks with your hands over your face, tasting the salt of your tears, and you know that this, this feeling, more than anything else you've ever experienced, was so meant to be.

Well, this is just a tiny, little taste of what it feels like to be the Universe, at all times.

Sure I cry. Whenever you do.

TOGA! TOGA! TOGA!

What, you think the Universe doesn't have toga parties?

Believe me, here it never ends!

The homecoming parties are really crazy!
Old loves and friendships are rekindled and spontaneous
enlightenment is passed around like, well, like you know what.

And then, there are the after parties . . . our favorites! Real
hoedowns for the most brilliant, radiant, and illuminated souls
in our midst. Fearless beings willing to further the collective
consciousness by delving into a kaleidoscope of emotions.
Embarking upon the greatest adventure ever imagined into the
sacred, hallowed jungles of time and space, where illumination
is taken to dazzling new levels and salvation guaranteed, not for
what they might do with their lives, but for simply
seeing them through.

These are the Bon Voyage Parties.

We owe you BIG.

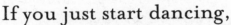

If you just start dancing,

I can assure you, by the powers vested in me (more than you could ever imagine), the music will be added. As will the partners, the giant disco ball, and whatever else you like.

But I must warn you, "start" is not to be confused with "start, and then stop to see if anything happens." Nope, that's "I'm scared, tired, and not sure of what I really want." I mean "start" as in "never stop, never look back, because even if I've made a 'mistake,' at least I still get to dance."

Do your thing, and I'll do mine.

Cha, cha, cha.

Sometimes, when it seems

your wings have suddenly and unexpectedly been clipped, maybe, just maybe, there's more to learn by staying where you are.

Maybe not.

You decide.

It's one kind of victory

to slay a beast, move a mountain, and cross a chasm.

But it's another kind altogether to realize that the beast and the mountain and the chasm were of your own design.

I keep telling 'em

that it's a jungle out there; that time and space isn't a place for "scaredies"; that toes are stubbed, hearts are broken, and dreams can seem to be shattered into a million pieces. I tell 'em that the illusions are so captivating, they won't even remember who they really are. And that the emotions can be so painful, at times they might fleetingly wish they were dead.

But it's like, that just makes them want to go even more.

Adventurers.

You bad.

What part of "visualize"
do you think most people misunderstand?

Or don't they do it, just once a day, for five minutes a day,
because they've yet to realize that whatever it is they
most want lies only a little thinking away?

"Can you hear me now?"

*Just once a day, for five minutes a day, followed by a little
"preparing the way," and you, too, could sing like Madonna, golf like Tiger,
and waltz like Matilda.*

Whatever you're going

to do today, please, do it to the best of your ability. As if it was all that mattered; as if it was all you had; and as if your very happiness depended upon it. Because these are among the very truths you came here to learn.

It is understandably human nature

to see yourself as small.

Until you stop seeing yourself as just human.

Should be easy for you . . .

You are pure energy: infinite, inexhaustible, and irresistible.

Well, by this point in the day,

if my calculations are correct, I expect you've already begun thinking of yourself as "mere mortal." Somewhat alone, a little bit confused, and responsible for figuring out how to make your life take off.

So . . . just thought I'd send you a reminder that at this very moment, there are a million eyes upon you, grateful for your courage; that you already know all you need to know; and that whether or not you can see it, you're already soaring.

Bravo.

Do you know how

to give folks what they most, most, most want from you
without even asking them what it is?

In all regards, just be yourself.

That's what they were after when they manifested
you into their lives.

Whoa!

You are, truly, one of a kind—and I would know.

The thing that most forget

while dreamily looking off into the horizon for the ship of
their dreams is that such ships never sail in but are
actually built beneath their very feet.

Get my drift?

A Manifestation Tip

from your friend the Universe:

Feeling gratitude in advance, before you even receive, as if you
already had, whether for direction or abundance or anything else,
opens the floodgates.

Did you catch the emphasis on feeling?

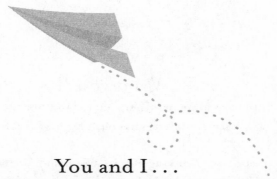

You and I . . .

we're older than the sun, wiser than the moon, and deeper than
the depths of space. We've always been together, we'll always be
together, and until thy Kingdom comes and we are known as
One, nothing will ever change this.

Whatever you can imagine, I can make happen. Whatever you
want, I already have. And for as long as you have thoughts to
think, dreams to weave, and seeds to sow, NOTHING,
for us, will be impossible.

What I'm trying to get at is, whatever you now want,
I think we can handle it.

Your dreams are what I've dreamed for you.

Was it you?!

We have some new "help" here, and our incoming
correspondence has been kind of garbled.

Someone was thinking big, I mean *really* big, and now the
entire Universe has been thrown into action, aligning players,
circumstances, and coincidences that will miraculously fall into
just the right place at just the right time. It's changed everything,
absolutely everything. The world will never be the same.

Actually, this happens with your every thought.

But if it was you, did you mean joy when you said toy? Sounded
like you wanted every toy?

Either way, consider it done, just let us know.

Tallyho,*
The Universe

PS—What are you gonna do with a piece of earth?

*Tallyho! (British for "After the fox!";
Adventurese for "Until we meet again . . .")

I just can't think of anything more

important to tell you than "Congratulations, outstanding, well done!" You are now, officially, the person you once dreamed you'd become.

Your courage and persistence have become as legendary as your cooking.

Just because all things

are possible, doesn't mean you're supposed to do all things.

Besides, it's not as if you aren't going to live forever.

Funny . . . If you were to repeat

the following phrase every single hour on the hour, or even just
once every single day, for months or years, what do you think
would eventually happen?

"I'm so sleepy, I'm just so tired, it's all I can do to stay awake . . ."

I know, I know, you're way beyond this. But here's a twist: What
if, while bright-eyed and wide-awake, feeling like you were in the
best shape of your life, brimming with vitality, you began with the
above mantra, what would happen then?

Okay, okay, so you're an old soul. But what if these things weren't
said while in a deep, meditative state, in an absolutely quiet
room? Would the results still be debilitating?

All right, Guru, I think I'm about to "get" you,
but first one more tease.

What if you didn't read another book on the "nature of reality"?
Didn't bother to hire a coach? Or follow a role model?
And you totally blew off the concepts of practicing, discipline,
and sacrifice? Would your sleepy mantra still
have any effect on you?

Oh my, I think I've done it! Have you ever before realized how ridiculously easy it is to transform your life? That no matter how unhappy you are today, or how deep in debt, or how bruised and tattered, or how unhealthy, or how lost, or how lonely . . . you already possess all the power, wisdom, and experience necessary to begin radically transforming your life by wisely choosing the words you speak, in spite of all evidence to the contrary?

Tallyho, abundant, triumphant, and happy soul.

Yeah, yeah, I know, I know you weren't born yesterday. And now you know that you "feel like a million bucks," that everything you "touch turns to gold," that you always "say the right thing at the right time," that "life is easy and fun," that your "path is clear," and that you "know exactly what to do" even if you can't yet "see" it.

Of course it's hard at first.
It's always hard at first.

You're going where you've never gone before in the jungles of
time and space. Cutting and hacking and slicing your way through
the thick, clinging bush.

And though the scenery may seem like it never changes,
the day will come when, from high on a new plateau, you'll look
back in total awe—amazed at the distance covered, the perils faced,
and the heights attained, overcome by the inevitability of it all,
bursting with pride, and struck most by the realization that
the only true dangers you ever faced were during the times
you felt like giving up or settling for less.

Yikes!
The Universe

*And you're also gonna laugh like a hyena when you see that the tigers were
made of paper and the lions were only me.*

Have you heard my Tarzan
impersonation? He taught me himself!

I love, love, love impersonations. I do a great Jane, too.
You'd never know it wasn't really her, believe me.

Actually, there isn't a soul on the planet that I haven't "done."
And when I say "done," I mean "hang ten, all out, the Full
Monty." Sometimes I get so carried away that I actually forget I'm
the Universe! I hate when that happens. Quite the juxtaposition,
if you can picture it. In one moment I'm the alpha and the
omega, and everything in between. And in the next I'm yearning,
pining, and dreaming poetically that one day, yes, one day,
just maybe, if I work hard enough, if I'm good enough, if I'm
not asking for too much, and if it's right for all concerned, my
dreams will come true.

Can you imagine?

Me?

You?

Actually, if you understood

the extraordinary gifts every single challenge in your life
makes possible, even inevitable, you'd celebrate your challenges,
new and old alike, as the omens they are of new beginnings,
spectacular change, and enhanced superpowers.

Perfect for where you are, huh?

Any kind of "superpowers" you can imagine . . .

Do it your way

and you'll win the attention, and the respect, of the whole world.

Not that you need it.

There are no finish lines in life,

yet perpetually seeking them, in terms of the quick fix, the big win, or a home run, serves only to remind you of what's missing, reinforcing the imagined lack. However, when one stops looking exclusively for results and embraces the journey as it is, the days will soon be innumerable when, looking back, you'll marvel at the distance covered.

Heigh-ho, and away . . .

It only seems to take a long time when you're looking for finish lines.

In your wildest dreams,

did you ever expect it would seem so real?

That your pains and sorrows would cut so deep, and that your
joys and laughter would feel so sublime?

No, I didn't think so, because one can't know, until they go,
which is why you're there. To feel the emotions that can only be
known by immersing yourself in the illusions of have and have
not. Because in time and space, no matter how much you have,
there's always more, and no matter how much you lack, there's
always less. Therefore, by simply being there, no matter what you
do, or who you become, or how much you think you gain or lose,
your purpose will be achieved.

To the winner's circle...

*The slate is otherwise blank; your thoughts, still, invariably become the things and
events of your life. And just as much can be learned by living in wealth
and abundance as without . . . So, let's do wealth and abundance.*

It's not the size of your dreams

that determines whether or not they come true, but the size of the actions you take that implies their inevitable arrival.

Your greatest admirer,
The Universe

And just so you know . . . the bigger the dream, the bigger the action.

Whoohoooooo! Great news!

Everything, absolutely everything you've ever wanted,
now lies within reach!

Of course . . . you still have to reach.

Hey, you have to admit, that's a pretty small price for "everything."

It's like there are countless

rooms in the mansion of your mind.

Some lavishly appointed and others quite spartan.
Rooms bursting with their own creative energies that draw you
into action. And others that make you feel frightened, angry, or
resentful the moment you've entered them. There are rooms that
inspire hope and foster new relationships. And others filled with
memories of what's already come to pass and
of dreams that never did.

It's like the more time you spend in any given room, gazing
from its windows, the more the outside world begins to justify,
reinforce, and in every case, resemble it.

And it's like most people just think they find themselves,
at any given point in a day, in one room or another without ever
realizing that every second of every day, they consciously choose
which room to hang out in.

Really, dear, it is your house...
But just a fig leaf?

Persistence, persistence, persistence.

On the surface it might just seem like physical flailing, but spiritually, you're speaking directly to me and you're saying, "You hear me, and you hear me good! There ain't no way I'm doing without. I refuse to accept 'maybe,' 'sort of,' or 'not yet.' I am the power, the glory, and the way. My words quicken the ether, my actions fulfill their prophecy, and thy Kingdom come on earth, as it is in heaven . . ."

And frankly, when confronted with such clarity . . . such style . . . such finesse, it makes my knees go wobbly and I'm like putty in your hands.

Rock on, rock on.

Do you know

what it's going to feel like when the day comes and everything
you now want has come to pass? When you're living in total
abundance, in perfect health, looking fabulous, with friends and
laughter wherever you go?

It's going to feel like, "Yeah . . . of course."

That's how well I know you.

Sometimes, not always, but sometimes,

being logical doesn't negate the magic, it stirs it up,
because not all miracles hide in the unseen.

Don't be afraid to do the obvious . . . really well.

Sometimes miracles even hang around, waiting for you to call, write, or show up.

You know what's kind of wild?

At this very crossroads of time and space, more than ever before,
there are so many billions of people yearning to awaken and
understand the truth about themselves, their divinity,
and the magic.

You know what else is kind of wild? Just as this need arose,
simultaneously, all over the world, there have appeared the
greatest teachers, though in far smaller numbers, who have ever
graced your plane. Those who are actually living these truths,
leading with the example of their lives, and healing those in need
through simple conversation.

Want to know what's even more unbelievable?
That you sometimes consider yourself more of the student.

Nope, don't worry, it hasn't affected your performance. You're already a legend.

If I were a business professor
and you were my student, today's lesson might sound like this:
Class . . . class . . . C-L-A-A-A-S-S!

In the "real" world, it's better to have loved and lost, tried and
failed, dreamed and missed, than to sit out your turn in fear.
Because the loss, the failure, and the miss, however painful, are
like temporary market adjustments, soon forgotten. Whereas the
love, the adventure, and the dream are like investments that, for
the rest of your life and beyond, never stop paying dividends.

Now, who brought me an apple?

Dr. Love

*Right you are! "How can you lose something you're still capable of giving?
How can you fail if you haven't stopped trying? And how can you miss, as long as
you're still aiming?"*

It's as if when you move, I move.

When you reach, I reach. And when you go the extra mile,
I clear the way . . . but not one single moment sooner.

Which is why, before you commit, things can sometimes
look pretty scary.

"Just like that."

A heartfelt compliment

given for no other reason than because it's meant,
is never, ever forgotten.

You've got the power.

*And that's not just because I move in the lips that speak them,
but also in the ears that hear.*

Hup! Stop! No! No! No!

Thinking about "how," weren't you?
How you're going to get from "here to there" kind of thoughts.
The cursed hows. Bummer, huh?

There's nothing quite as demoralizing in the human experience
as trying to use your brain to map the unseen, because
immediately you sense it's hopeless . . . and you're right!

You can't map the unseen! But I can.

You just need to define "there" and get busy doing what you can
in every direction that feels right, *though insisting upon none.*

Do the logical things (like knocking on doors and turning over
stones). Do the spiritual things (like visualizing and taking
catnaps). And leave the accidents, coincidences,
and spontaneous illumination to me.

In a way, it's almost like throwing paint on the wall, and then
trusting me to connect the dots. Because I will, and the resulting
masterpiece will blow you away. I promise.

After all, who do you think gave the
Mona Lisa *her smile?*

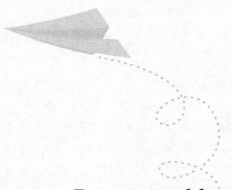

Dreams are like that . . .

Most of the time you don't even know how close you are,
until after they've come true.

Sometimes, even, the very day before they come true,
it still feels like they're a million miles away.

Something to remember.

*I think it works like this because if you knew how close you really were, you'd
probably get so nervous that your legs would shake, your voice would break, and
you'd come so undone that we'd have to call for a "do-over."*

Changing one's life is easy

and there are lots of ways to go about it,
though all exact some sort of price:

Pinpointing invisible, limiting, self-sabotaging beliefs—
extremely demanding on brain cells and much easier to do
if you have a friend who channels the dead, but either way,
it'll keep you busy for the rest of your life.

Discovering what occurrences in the past have misprogrammed
you—a therapist can help, though expensive if you don't have
insurance, but you can both pretend you're a complex
person and that if it wasn't for your childhood,
you'd have the perfect life.

Distinguishing between those who really love you and those
who just wish to use you—super tricky, and may destroy perfectly
good relationships, but with a good lawyer you can laugh all
the way to the bank while accepting little or no responsibility
for your own happiness.

These are just a few of the most popular and widely written about methods. Of course, you could also just begin imagining and moving toward the life of your dreams, treating everyone with kindness, and assuming all is well—profoundly and radically effective for both short- and long-term gains, but totally lacking in drama, requires solo efforts, and is much too easy for most people to take seriously.

Your move,
The Universe

The easiest way

to avoid letdowns and disappointments, is . . .

No, it's not lowering your standards.
That's quitting.

No, it's not releasing expectations.
That's an old wives' tale.

And no, it's not relinquishing all mortal desires.
That's an Eastern religion.

It's never tricking yourself into thinking that your happiness is
dependent upon the things and events of time and space,
or what other people think, say, and do.

And no, it's never really had anything to do with chocolate.
That was the Cookie Monster.

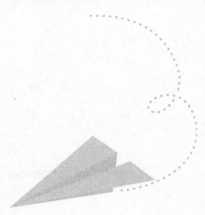

Ever wonder how much patience

you should have with someone before you lose your temper?

Infinite.

But careful, now. That doesn't mean you have to wait for them, stay with them, or hang around them. Lord, no. It just means that for as long as you choose to keep them in your life, understanding them, not changing them, is everything.

You couldn't be freer.

Anger is one of enlightenment's
many barometers.

Basically, the more you have of one,
the less you have of the other.

Yessiree, "Bob."

Don't get mad, get smart.

Not desire, but expectation,
unlocks wheels, parts seas, moves mountains,
and changes everything.

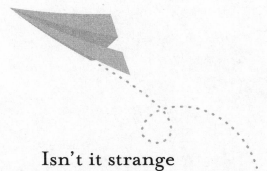

Isn't it strange

how you can find metaphors for life absolutely everywhere?

I mean, here I sit at the coffee shop and everything seems to be a
parody of time and space. The smiles and warmth that greet you
around every corner mirror your own.

After you place your order and do what you know to do,
you expectantly trust you'll be served. Worrying about
the hows is ludicrous.

And over at the sidebar, the really sweet stuff . . . is free.

*Whoops . . . there . . . right there . . . lower . . . You've got some foam on the tip
of your nose. And yes, we have coffee here. We have everything here
(we had it first, I might add).*

Believe me, I know all about it.

I know the stress. I know the frustration.
I know the temptations of time and space.

We worked this out ahead of time.
They're part of the plan. We knew this stuff might happen.

Actually, you insisted they be triggered whenever you were ready
to begin thinking thoughts you've never thought before.

Good on you.

If you know what you want,

if you've made up your mind, if you can see it, feel it, and move toward it in some small way every single day . . . *it has to happen.*

Talking a lot about something

that bothers you is a pretty good sign that you've got something huge and profoundly liberating to learn.

Whooohooooo!

That is, if you can catch yourself, turn within, and yearn for illumination.

A Community Service Reminder
from the Universe.

YOU RULE.

Your gifts are innumerable.
Your insights are profound.
Your choices are endless.
Your touch is healing.
Your thoughts become things.
Your power is indescribable.

And you are loved and adored, on a moment-to-moment basis
more than you can now understand.

YOU RULE.

So I was thinking...

I know you know that there's the "you" that you know
you are—adventurous, good-looking, and fun to be around.
And I know you know that there's another part of "you" in the
unseen who you've kind of temporarily forgotten—who completes
you, loves you, and knows what's really going on.

Well, how'd you like it if I removed the veils?
Just for a second? Gave you a glimpse of who that special,
divine, otherworldly essence is, so that you might at last begin to
comprehend how extraordinary, sublime,
and divine you really are?

Okay... It's me. The *entire* Universe.

Surprise, surprise, surprise.

What?
You were expecting some little Tinker Bell?

To err on the side of generosity,

patience, and kindness . . . is not to err.

Because no little thing slips by me that isn't returned
bigger and better.

Things only get better.

Yeah, I know, not everyone will be ready for that one . . .

But they're getting better.

What's worse than being human
and hearing fingernails scrape a chalkboard?

Being the Universe and hearing "May I? Can I? Will I?"
instead of "Thank you. Thank you. Thank you."

Makes my face squinch up.

*I'd even prefer
"Hubba! Hubba! Hubba!"*

This might sound a bit conceited,

but there's a part of me that's human, too (if you know what I mean). I'm a big-picture person, and from here I can see all of you. ALL that you've been through, every decision you've ever made, and I know exactly where you're headed. I know your every hope, dream, and fear. I've seen you at your "best" and your "worst," on good days and bad.

And I gotta confess, I couldn't possibly be prouder of who I've become.

Yeah, me.

When the choice is to hurt or be hurt.
Cheat or be cheated. Violate or be violated.
Always, always, always choose the latter.

Trust me.

Besides, predicaments like these don't just happen.

Let's see, last time I checked
you were still a forever being with as many second chances
and new romances saved up as there are stars in the night sky;
whose thoughts fly on wings, whose dreams become things, and
for whom all the elements bow.

Just in case you were wondering.

*Where is it? Where is it?! Have you seen your future lately . . . ?
Oh, there it is! Spinning in the palm of your hand.*

It's not a matter of feeling worthy

of love, friends, health, or wealth. Or of appreciating what you
already have. Or even of learning to love yourself. These don't
have to come first. You don't have to wear a halo
to manifest the changes you want.

It's simply a matter of understanding that if you do your part,
visualize, prepare the way, and act "as if" without looking back
over your shoulder for quick results, what you want must be
added unto you, as will the feelings of worthiness, appreciation,
and loving your hot-bodied self.

You're prequalified to rock the world.
There are no other rules.

Besides, feeling unworthy does not make you so.

Do you know
what's already happened this month?

A million Beethovens were born.
A million Frida Kahlos.
A million Einsteins.
A million Florence Nightingales.
A million Martin Luther King Jrs.
And a million Rosa Parks, to name just a few.

Each as capable of moving mountains, touching lives, and leaving
the world far better than they found it.

And so you can just imagine how all of us "here" watch in
anticipation to see which ones will have the courage to do
whatever little they can each day, with what little they've got, from
where they are, before their baby steps turn into
giant leaps for all.

It's so in you.

Best I can figure,

the reason some get down-and-out, lose motivation,
and watch too much TV is that they've somehow forgotten just
how fast things can change, and they've yet to discover
just how good they can get.

Even you are going to be surprised.

Not that I don't check in on The Late Show *every now and then, myself.*

Much is said

about the lust for material things, so if I may add to the
chorus . . . Go for it!

After all, matter is pure spirit, only more so.

To put this tactfully . . .

If you don't start doing stuff to prepare for all the fun changes that are about to take place in your life, j-e-e-e-z, I just don't know what might happen.

But I'm darn sure I know what won't.

I'm not from the IRS, but I'm here to help.

I'm also crazy about you!

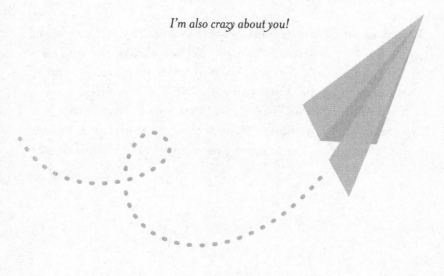

The slate's been wiped clean,

the past has released its grip, and before you sparkles eternity
yearning for direction. All that now stands between you and the
life of your dreams is just one teeny, tiny, gentle little rule. Only
one condition, prerequisite, principle that matters.

It's not love. It's not God. It's not fate, or luck, or karma. It's not
complicated or esoteric, and you needn't sacrifice, plead, or pray
to invoke it. It's the only rule that's ever existed, and it's the only
one that ever will exist. No reality can exist in its absence. For its
mere existence, you are. With its existence, the power, the light,
and the way are revealed. It's your purpose to discover it, and it's
your destiny to master it. It's the beginning, the middle, and the
end. The alpha and the omega. The be-all and end-all of every
wish, desire, and dream, and you are its keeper.

This caveat of all caveats is that absolutely nothing can be anything
until it is first imagined. Thoughts become things, nothing else
does. And so, it's the thoughts you choose from here on out
that will become the things and events of your life, forevermore.
It is written in stone. There's no other way. It's your ticket to
anywhere you can dream of. Your passport to abundance, health,
and friendships. The key to the palace of your wildest dreams.

Your thoughts, and your thoughts alone, will set you in motion. Your thoughts will yield the inspiration, creativity, and determination you need. Your thoughts will orchestrate the magic and inspire the Universe. Your thoughts will carry you to the finish line if you just keep thinking them. Never give up. Never waver, doubt, or ask.

Aim high.

That you're even reading this Note, that you're able to read it through, means you are so close. So extraordinarily close. The hardest work has been done. Your inner battles have already been won. The lessons have already been learned. The journey, now, is for home.

You're so deserving. You're ready.
It's all that stands between you and the life of your dreams.

If ever there was a symbiotic relationship,
you know, like leafhoppers and meat ants, clownfish and
Ritteri sea anemones, the Egyptian plover bird and the crocodile,
each of which thrives because of the existence of the other,
it's me and you, babe.

Include me in your every thought, as I do you.

You have something in your teeth.

Of course, I think unceasingly of you.
You threatened to eat me alive if I ever forgot.

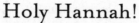

Holy Hannah!

I just realized there is no one else in the world like you. No one who has your sense of compassion. Your penetrating insights. And your extraordinary zest for life.

What was I thinking about?

Oh yeah, "my image."

We rock.

Thought it was too much to be coincidence. And while all the rest are in my image, too, somehow not a single one has quite your style and "savoir faire." Hmm...

It goes like this . . .

Whatever you're capable of summoning,
imagining, and moving toward, however feebly
to begin with, I am capable of delivering.

In expectation,
The Universe

Careful, now, 'cause you are gonna get it!

It's never, never, never

too late to give thanks in advance for the help
you stand in need of, as if you've already received it.

Because you just wouldn't believe how much I can
accomplish in no time at all, literally.

Thanks for listening.

See? It works.

In the time that it takes you

to read this short Note, you could have planted a new image
in your mind (anything you like, ideally with an emotional
charge), I could have reacted (realigning planets, people, and
the sort), and the floodgates would've begun trembling
violently as we'd have been drawn infinitely closer to
manifesting the vision you'd chosen.

Fortunately, there's still time.

It doesn't have to be hard or take a lot of time.
Visualize, it's the least you can do.

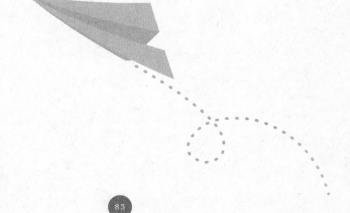

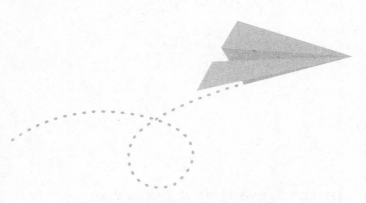

One hundred years from now,

it will not matter what was in your bank account, what kind of
car you drove, or what style of home you lived in.

On the other hand, since one of the reasons you're in time and
space is to understand that you do, indeed, have dominion over
all things . . . nailing these early on would be way cool.

*And what better way to be important in the eyes of a child than to live your power
so that they might observe and learn to live theirs?*

Is it just me,
or does it all seem far too good to possibly be true?

And among other things, how many different flavors of chocolate does one really need?

There's always a way.
Though chances are, it's not the one that first comes to mind.

Commit only to the end result, drop the "cursed hows," and be unfettered by closed doors, dashed hopes, and broken promises.

In all tests of character,

when two viewpoints are pitted against each other,
in the final analysis, the thing that will strike you the most is not
who was right or wrong, strong or weak, wise or foolish . . . but
who went to the greater length in considering
the other's perspective.

Don't you agree?

Well, yeah, I did mean the final, final analysis, but you'll see,
that one really counts big.

You know, it seems a shame
that for many, life doesn't seem fair.

But perhaps that's one of the reasons you were summoned:
to make life a little more bearable for them until they learn how
fair it is, and so that they can then do the same for others.

So . . .
Did they get a good deal, or what?

And when I say "perhaps," it's just diplomacy.

There's nothing wrong

with wanting "more."

It means you're alive and well.

Actually, you're "supposed" to want more.

Ye-e-e-h-a-a-a-w! FRIDAY!

Do you know what that means?

It means you've still got time.
It means it's still your turn.
It means I can't stop loving you.

Ye-e-e-h-a-a-a-w! MONDAY!

Do you know what that means?

It means you're dreaming. In a place where your thoughts
become the things and events of your life. And in this dream
you're about to manifest, yet again, a brand-new adventure
framed by the illusion of seven days. And any villains or heroes
you encounter this week; any highs or lows; strikeouts,
base hits, or home runs; Mack Daddies, Sugar Babies,
or Oprah Winfreys . . . will be of your own design.

Ah! If you "do" an Oprah, please tell her about these Notes!

Ye-e-e-h-a-a-a-w! TUESDAY!
Just kidding.

Ahem . . .
Even though this will seem like a lie:
No one can be lied to who has not first, somehow,
some way, lied to themselves.

Self-deception is really the only kind there is.

Have you heard the one about
the little boy who asked his mom why people don't fly?

She told him, "It's mostly because they forget they have wings."

Sorry, not really funny, but I just didn't want you to
forget about yours.

To the stars,
The Universe

Hey! I've been looking

over all my old photos, and yes, you guessed it,
you look absolutely smashing.

But honestly, if you don't mind my saying so,
you're never quite as beautiful in a photograph—mine or
anyone else's—as you are in person. Not even close.

The odd quiver of your lip, the sparkle in your eye, and the
hidden "question mark," sometimes, when you smile. The
confidence behind your laughter, the concern behind your tears,
and the unpredictability of your wit.

The reassurance of your glance, the easiness of your presence,
and the "junk in your trunk." I wouldn't change one single thing.
But you guessed that, too, huh?

Isn't it strange, though, how some still expect to see all that
when looking at a photo of themselves, or just staring,
motionless, into a mirror?

Maybe if they at least waved?

If anyone should ever ask

if you're enlightened . . .

ALWAYS SAY YES!

Same goes for being healthy, wealthy,
and loved beyond imagination.

Got it?
The Universe

Your word is your wand.

Wow! What an incredible year!

Lots of firsts, tons of breakthroughs, countless miracles.
Stones overturned, doors unlocked, and journeys just begun.
It feels like I've waited an eternity for all that's now happening.
(Actually, I have.)

Do you have any idea how many millenniums, billenniums,
trillenniums have gone by without you in the world? Thinking
the kind of thoughts you now think, doing the kind of stuff you
now do, and illuminating all the nooks and crannies (n-o-o-o-o,
I didn't almost say "crooks and grannies") of the planet
I couldn't otherwise reach? Too many.

Thanks, and have a great day!

Your fellow Adventurer,
The Universe

Well worth the wait.
But next time I create a reality, would you mind, terribly,
being among the first to visit?

Whoohoo!

The script for the most amazing time in your life is nearing
perfection! We're so excited and happy for you.
Bravo. Bravo. Bravo.

It's complete with friends and laughter, wealth and abundance,
health and harmony. And best of all, there are going to be some
really neat surprises. BIG surprises! Really HUGE, Texas style.

And you're gonna say, "B-bu...but...I...I...I...
H-Ho...How? Never in all my life have I imagined such
outrageousness! All my expectations have been exceeded! Never
have I dreamed of being so blessed!"

And we're gonna say, "Oh, yes you did."
And you're gonna say, "Oh, no I didn't."
And we'll say, "Did."
And you'll say, "Didn't."

And then we'll remind you of those occasions when you simply saw yourself happy. Visualizing euphoric happiness, bypassing the details. Smiling from ear to ear in your mind's eye, pumping your fist, dialing your friends' cell phone numbers with shaking fingers, happy tears running down your face, when you left all of the "hows" to the Universe.

And you're gonna say, "Oh."

And we're gonna say, through tears of our own, "Nice hows, huh?"

"Action!"

Have you ever thought of writing for the movies?

Whoops...

ever since I began handing out wings and giving dominion to those made in my image, there seems to be the misconception that happiness will come from doing, being, and having *it all* when actually, as you well know, it's the other way around.

You want to tell 'em?

And, yes. You do have wings.

Remember when it was really fun

to catch raindrops on your tongue, walk under archways because
they were there, and roll around in the sand at the beach?

To go all the way to the store for a tiny treat, lie on the grass
looking for "God" in the clouds, and make scary
monster faces in the mirror?

To watch the stars because they were winking at you,
count the flowers in the garden by the door, and to put
Cocoa Puffs up your nose?

Well, I'm happy to inform you, most of it still is.

Ah-h-h-h-h-h-h-h...

Whoohoooo, you're alive!

Rule #1 for Giving:

Expect not that your Kingdom will come, or your bounty
will be multiplied, via the recipient of your kindness.

Drives me absolutely, totally crazy—and severely
limits my options.

Besides, I've always preferred surprising you.

If you only knew how many
miracles you've already performed, nothing would ever again
overwhelm you, frighten you, or seem impossible.

And you'd begin admiring yourself, as we always have.

Aha!

Do you know what your thoughts did last week?!
Oh, yes you do.

They became the things and events of this week. The things you
thought would be difficult became difficult; easy became easy;
boring became boring; and fun became fun. Where you thought
there might be surprises, you were surprised. And where you
thought there might be "land mines," there were "land mines."

Bravo! You can add last week to the list of your
most creative accomplishments.

Now, can you guess what your thoughts this week are going to do?

Please, choose every single one of them as if nothing else mattered.

It's me, the Universe.
I've got good news and bad news.

The good news is that you've passed the audition!
Yee-haa! You've earned your wings! You're a certified, bona fide
Being of Light, capable of transcending all fears and manifesting
all dreams. From here on out, you have but to dwell upon
what you want, and I must bring it forth.

The bad news . . . is that this message was supposed to have
reached you eons and eons ago.

Sorry.

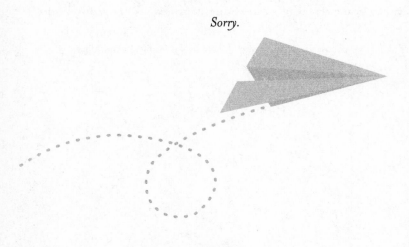

Of course dreams come true.

Just look around you. Out the window. Down the hall.
Into the mirror. These were all once dreams of mine.

And I had a whole lot less to work with.

As you've probably deduced

by now, I don't think in terms of reasonable or unreasonable,
likely or unlikely, possible or impossible.
I merely figure out the "hows."

Guess what that leaves you with?

Let's give them something to talk about.

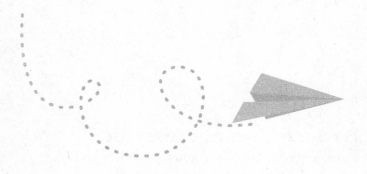

You know how

when you visualize something every day, to such a degree that
you can literally taste its reality? And you believe in the
likelihood of its manifestation with all your heart and soul?
And as often as you think of it, in at least some small way, you
prepare for its arrival? Yet still absolutely nothing happens?

Right! That's impossible.

Just do your part, I'll do mine, and everything has to change.

There are some folks

who think that life isn't fair, and to them I say, "Touché!"

Obviously, they see themselves as unlimited Beings of Light for whom all things are possible. They recognize that their thoughts become things, giving rise not only to dreams, but to worlds. And they appreciate that their very existence in time and space proves that they're loved beyond imagination.

Yes, these are the folks who understand that with dominion over all things, the cards of life are indeed stacked in their favor.

N'est-ce pas?
You couldn't be more favored.

Persistence is priceless,
but its value lies in doing, doing, doing,
not in waiting, waiting, waiting.

Okay? Okay? Okay?

The Universe

Not that you were hanging around for someone, some way, or somehow!

It totally flips me out.
People talk to me, they ask me stuff, they show me things,
yet so rarely do they ever expect a reply.

Am I invisible or something?

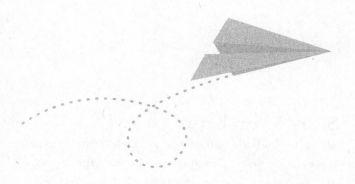

You need never doubt
that I tirelessly conspire on your behalf.

Because if it hasn't occurred to you yet, I need you as much as you need me. To show me the way, to give me each day, and to go where I couldn't otherwise go.

Amen,
The Universe

You complete me.

Scary? You bet it's scary!

Package yourself up into a little ball of energy. Deliberately forget
that you're everywhere, always, and at once—the sun, the moon,
and the stars. Expose yourself, as a tiny baby, no less, to the
minds of those who are as lost as you—however well meaning.
Adopt their beliefs. Play their games. Spend much of your life
living by their rules. And trust that you just happen to notice that
your thoughts still, invariably, without exception, become
the things and events of your life.

Have faith that you're open-minded enough to accept that you're
the cause, if you believe in effects; accept responsibility for
everything that has, or has not, ever happened to you. So that,
finally, you recognize your unmitigated superpowers,
claim them, and rock the world!

I'm terrified. It may well be my finest work.
How will I follow up on creating a reality like that?

Yes, we'll think of something adventurous.

Actually, if it were any easier,
it wouldn't be worth it.

You'll see.

Thanks for being there,
even through the "hard" times.

And sorry if they've ever seemed like too much.
But I'm pretty sure it was you, after all, who said,
"I want it all—no matter the cost."

You power shopper, you.
The Universe

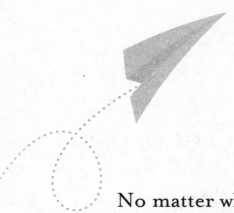

No matter what else
you might feel or think, it's working,
flawlessly, magically, and without exception.

Your thoughts, beliefs, and expectations are the sole cause of the
effects of your life. And while this may give you pause and have
you wondering why you've not yet met with some of the successes
you've sought, let it also empower you as you remember that the
floodgates must fly open and the Kingdom must be revealed at
the precise moment when you release whatever else you might
have felt or thought about it not working.

Lots of people wonder . . .
Fewer take the time to really think.

But I'll be darned; sometimes I think I could count on the fingers
of my hand how many actually visualize the life of their dreams,
as if their dreams had *already* come true, every single day,
for just five minutes or so.

Do it till you're satisfied.

Yeah, big hands, lots of fingers, but still.

Have you heard about
the "Bewitching Hour"?

Actually, it's top secret, so I'll whisper.

Every single morning, ever since time began, before the sun even rises, the drums start beating, the choirs start singing, the energy starts rising, and every single soul who has ever lived scurries around the plane of manifestation as a chanting begins . . . And gets louder and louder . . . And goes faster and faster until . . . a feverish pitch is reached and the celestial skies part with a clap of thunder, revealing billions upon billions of the most beautiful angels you have ever seen. Flying down from the heavens, some with wings outstretched, others with wings pointed back. Darting, diving, banking, and rolling—some so fast they're only a blur— while others seem to float by as if catching what remained of a midsummer night's breeze.

Every one of them a reflection of the greatest, the loveliest, and the highest I've ever imagined. Every one of them a messenger of hope, and peace, and joy; healers and teachers, comforters and creators. And every one of them about to greet a brand-new day in time and space with a morning yawn, sleepy eyes, and the power to ROCK THE WORLD.

This is the "Bewitching Hour." Shhhh...

If you listen really hard, you can still hear the drums.

Hosanna in the highest.

Nice inverted-triple-axel-gallactica this morning.
Seems like just yesterday when you were still somersaulting
the whole way—doesn't it?

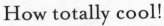

How totally cool!
Last night we were dreaming together!

Do you remember? Soaring in and out of mile-high clouds.
Walking upon lazy lakes and raging rivers. Manifesting gold coins
from our blue-jean pockets. Reaching out to the many who are
only just now discovering that thriving is their natural state, that
abundance is their birthright, and that friends, guides,
and admirers are only ever a nod away.

Shoot. You were right.
You said you wouldn't remember a thing.

Well, that's okay. I was right, too.
I said that those you helped would never forget.
Just like when you're awake.

See you tonight,
The Universe

Ain't immortality grand?

Your balance

of wit, charm, and intelligence . . .
The measures of your endurance, strength, and stamina . . .
The depths of your sensitivity, passion, and leanings . . .
It's never, not ever, been done before.

Now, do you think these things were all proportioned
accidentally? Or do you think they were my idea, designed to take
me where others couldn't go?

Bingo.

*Well, yeah, kind of like that neat Mars rover, but on Earth,
without the glitches, and cuter.*

I'm hungry!
Hungry for adventure.
The adventure of love.

Tell you what: The more of it you give today to the least
deserving on your list, the more your life will change.

Here's the rub.
If it wasn't so flippin' simple—manifesting change,
finding happiness, living the life of your dreams—
I really do think more people would "get it."

Think, think, and let go.

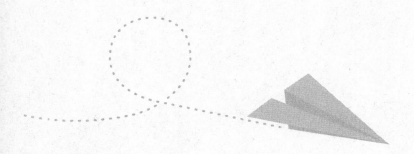

The thing about success

is that she often arrives at such a late hour that only the oddballs, freaks, and nuts (you know, the ones who continued believing, in spite of all worldly evidence to the contrary) remain to greet her.

A little weird is good.

The Universe

Well, she doesn't have to arrive so late, but sometimes that's also how long it takes before people stop fretting about whether or not she ever will.

It's not the dazzling voice

that makes a singer. Or clever stories that make a writer.
And it's not piles of money that make a tycoon.

It's having a dream and wanting to live it so greatly that one would
rather move with it and "fail" than succeed in another realm.

You so have what it takes.

At which point, of course, failure becomes impossible, joy becomes the measure of
success, and fitting into the jeans you wore back-in-the-day, inevitable.
Hubba, hubba.

Oh, they love me all right!
They really, really love me.

But sometimes I wonder if the reason they love me has anything to do with the thought that one day, just maybe, I'm going to be the spark, ignite the fire, and summon the magic that will make all of their dreams come true.

Yikes, are they ever going to be surprised when they find out that's their job?

Think not that today
foretells tomorrow, for it never has.

Same goes for the past.

Only you can do that.

Do you have any idea

how thoroughly, utterly, and completely I want the
very things you now want?

Well, let's just say that after my own visualizing, and expecting,
and acting with faith, then came you.

We're in this together.

Banzai—
The Universe

May you live ten thousand years!
(As if you haven't already.)

If it wasn't for needing you
there so much, I'd need you here.

"Thanks," on behalf of all those in your life right now
who are just too busy, or stressed, or sad to see how much
you add to theirs.

You know who I mean.

The Universe

I'm not wild about cloning, unless they're talking about you.

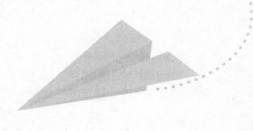

An enlightened soul

is not one to whom truth has been revealed, but one who has
summoned it. And not just when they've been driven by pain,
but when life's seas were as calm as glass.

But you have to admit it's kind of handy that way, pain.
Just worked out like that. Honest.

Release me,

release me to do your will. To move heaven and earth.
To orchestrate the players and summon the circumstances
that will change your life completely by doing your all-out
best, with today.

That's all the leg up I need.

With just a word from you,
just a word—I'm there.

No matter where "there" is. No matter what you want. No matter what you need. No matter where you've been. No matter where you're headed. No matter when you ask. No matter how you ask. No matter who's there with you. No matter who else you're thinking of. No matter what, no matter what, no matter what.

Please, believe me,
The Universe

And I travel with all the angels—every single one of them—
with just a word from you.

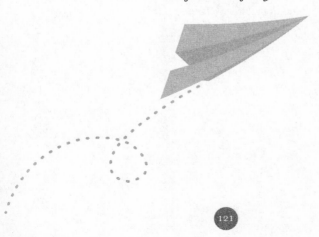

You have a track record here,
have you forgotten?

Little ... teensy ... tiny ...

That's how all of your present issues, challenges, and so-called
problems will one day soon appear. And then you'll wonder—one
hot summer's eve as you're floating lazily across your swimming
pool (hidden orchestra playing loudly in the background),
healthy, confident, and just beaming about your recent successes
in real estate; toned, sculpted, and tanned, carelessly splashing
your friends, telling jokes, and occasionally laughing so hard you
almost capsize—how you could've ever thought they were such a
big deal. I know you.

You call that thing a bathing suit?

Happily...
Between here and there, the only thing that matters
is what you think between now and then.

The past is simply what you choose to remember,
if you even choose to remember it.

You're not there to learn
how to make your thoughts become the things and events of your
life. Too hard, too complicated. B-o-r-i-i-i-n-g.
Leave that to me.

No, you're there to learn that they already do.
Every single one of them. Always have, always will.

How could it be easier?

If you were to ask me,

I'd probably say that the number one cause of loneliness in time
and space is not a lack of friends, but a lack of keeping busy.

I'd even go so far as to say that nine out of ten times the solution
to every crisis, challenge, or problem—in relationships, careers,
or otherwise—is to get busy.

Because when you get busy, you allow me to slide whatever you
most need—be it material, spiritual, or a new friend; answers,
ideas, or comfort—right under your big ol' nose.

The one time out of ten?
It's to first be still—and then get busy.

Beneath your luminous skin,

just behind the sparkle of your eyes, emanating from the depths of your soul, there's a fire-breathing dragon, possessing unimaginable strength, wisdom, and thoughts that reach out and sizzle every corner of the Universe.

A playful dragon. A fearless dragon. A good-looking dragon. Colossal, yet swift; spontaneous, yet clever; unreasonable, yet assured; outrageous, yet innocent; determined, yet patient; cautious, yet carefree; light, yet less filling.

A predator, guardian, and connoisseur of adventure.

And I think it's really cool how, lately, I'm seeing more and more of it come out. Gives new meaning to "hottie."

Oh, hi...
at least you're still talking to me.

Was just sitting here on the beach wondering whether or not the whole thing was a good idea in the first place, you know?

When the idea first dawned on me, it seemed like one heck of an adventure. Endless possibilities. Incomparable camaraderie.

A little bit of me in everyone (okay, a lot).
My style, my rhythm, my appetite for fun.

I had no idea people could feel so lost . . . So sad. So alone.

Well, this much I know for sure: next time I throw a "bring your out-of-body" party in the middle of the night, we won't turn off the music at the sound of the first alarm clock. Escorts will be provided upon reentry to avoid accidental body swapping. And illumination, guardianship, and inspiration shall be made available at all times for those who are confused, just like on earth, as long as they ask and expect to be heard.

Shake your tail feathas . . .
The Universe

What did you think I was talking about? By the way, loved your kilt. Where it fit.

Can you see me, right now?
Yes—I'm the light, and all it shines on.

Can you hear me?
Yep—every single sound, and the silence, too.

Can you feel me? Right now? In the air on your skin, under your feet, and in the palms of your hands? The tug at your heart, the rhythm it keeps, and the blood in your veins?

Right. Now, next time you have cause for alarm, see me. Next time you need absolutely anything, listen to me. And next time you feel all alone, remember you're not.

Once you make up your mind
to start something, commit to it, say "Yes!",
and never look back.

Do you have any doubt, any whatsoever, that I will not rush to
your side? That legions won't be summoned? That players won't
be drawn to your corner? Connections made? Circumstances
crafted? Dots connected? That the course of history won't be
irrevocably changed?

Good, I didn't think so.

I'd say you're ready.

Was that a "Yes!"?

Everything can change
so very, very fast.

And it usually does.

Whoohoooooooooo!

There's no predicament
that can't be turned into an advantage.

No foe who can't become a friend.

And no burden that cannot give you wings.

How fair is that?

Oh, shoot!

Did I remember to ask you to turn off the lights?
You know, in the "Hall of Records" after I showed you
where all the books written about you were?

Remember, not a word to anyone!
(Most don't believe in traversing time, yet,
and they'll think you're losing it.)

S-h-h-h-h . . .
The Universe

Told you. You put on quite a show, didn't you? Changed the bloomin' world.

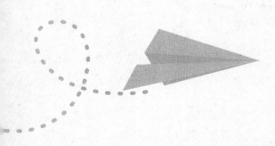

Well, enlightenment
is kind of like flying for the first time without wings.

Of course, there's the exhilaration, the happiness, and the intoxicating sense of freedom that's almost indescribable.

But there's also the subtle shock at what you now see as the inevitability of your accomplishment. The wonderment of how you hadn't seen this so clearly before, mingled with acceptance. And the dim recognition that it's part of some distant agreement you once made.

And, at last, as you come to your senses and finally think to gaze below, upon the tiny jewel you've called home for so long, you're struck with a jolt as you see it so magically and effortlessly suspended—floating—in space, and you realize, for the first time, *that even there you were flying all along.*

Up ahead!!!
There's a tree coming right at you!

Nothing you will ever do, be, or have,

no matter how stunning and spectacular, will ever compare to
your achievement of being here at all.

Yes, *your* achievement.

Amazing, though, how people will put off celebrating
the big stuff for the little stuff.

Don't wait.

Believe it or not,

if it weren't for your so-called issues, problems, and challenges,
there'd be no other way you could become even happier, cooler,
and more enlightened than you have ever been before.

Granted, you being even cooler boggles the mind.

You know those feelings of

euphoria, excitement, and inspiration that send your spirit soaring? Well, they're just me and all the angels, finally rushing through one of the many doors you've knocked upon, down the hall, and dancing into the light of your searching heart.

And those feelings of depression, sadness, and powerlessness that make you feel like you're carrying the weight of the world on your shoulders? They're us, too. Reminding you that there are still a few more doors to try.

Let's get this party started.

When it comes to "having it all,"
many fine, young souls take issue with the word "have."

They're concerned about the concept of ownership. Their soul is taunted by guilt for the pleasure it derives from material things. And they quiver at the thought of "others" having less than they have.

Of course, such righteous and selfless thoughts are a significant contributor to the creation of lack in a world of endless abundance, but they'll learn.

"Kids...!"

You want what you want

because you know it's possible. If it wasn't, you wouldn't.

This is powerful. Embrace it. For whatever else you believe or don't believe, this belief alone can take you the distance.

Please, want what you want.

Dreams don't come that can't be won.

As surely as the snow falls,

the winds rage, and the rivers run, so are you, minute by minute, day by day, inevitably drawn to all your heart's desires.

Sure beats thinking that you're just getting older.

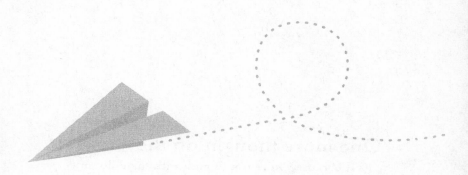

Do you think

having your own private little planet where you could have, do,
and be anything you dreamed of, with as many friends as you
choose, would be worth it, if the price of admission was to forget
how you got there so that you could discover
your throne, on your own?

All bow.

*You always were a trendsetter. But do you have any idea how many others I've had
to strike the same bargain with?*

One more thought on the "hows."

Just because you're not to mess with them doesn't
mean you're not to get busy doing all you can, with what
you've got, from where you are.

The difference is in how you see what you do: you don't do
all you can with an eye to hitting a home run, but with an
understanding that for each door you knock upon and every
stone you turn over, you're pitching the ball to me.

The more balls you pitch, the greater my options,
and the farther the balls will sail.

Batter up,
The Universe

*It's like, if you want me to do ALL I can (move mountains and that sort of thing),
you must do ALL you can (cast-your-bread sort of thing).*

The thing about pessimism . . .

about fearful thoughts . . . about limiting beliefs . . .
is that they really, really work.

Boo,
The Universe

Now, that's about as scary as things get in time and space!

Sometimes life

is like reading a book.

Days, weeks, even years just repeat themselves . . .
until you turn the page.

Letting go isn't giving up.
It's understanding that the best is yet to come.

Universal Personality Test:

Want to know how to tell whether you were born with the gift
to heal? Or perhaps if your strengths lie in leadership?
If you're a left- or right-brained individual? Whether or not
you're truly a people person? Whether or not, given your
beliefs... friends, laughter, and abundance will flow to
you effortlessly, or should be diligently sought after?

Just decide.

It's always worked before.

For just a moment,

can you imagine that on the day the earth was created,
I'd want to experience her in every imaginable form?

Good.

Now can you imagine that when it came to creating the animals,
I couldn't just pick one—but would want to soar through the skies,
swim in the oceans, and burrow in the fields?

Excellent. I had to be all of her animals, to experience
all of their secrets.

So when it came to having dominion over all things, it must now
be just as obvious that I had to be everyone.

And I am.

I walk in your shoes. Every day.

As much as I love my "job,"

I do have "my days."

Maybe you can help me out?

Tell me, what advice would you give a child who came
to you asking what their favorite color should be?

That no color is right or wrong? To follow their heart? That if
they wanted to, they could always change their mind later,
any number of times? That their happiness with their choice is
all that matters? Not to give it too much importance? That they
don't have to decide at all? That you approve
no matter what they choose?

My, you are good!

Now, what if they protested because they heard from friends that
there was a special color assigned to them at birth, their
soul-color. They felt that a numerology reading might shed some
light on their confusion. They wanted confirmation of their
choices through a zodiac chart, tea leaves, or a Ouija board. And
they asked if finding a new guru would be a good idea.

See?

Sorry to lay that on you. I'm just fishing around for some
new answers to the bazillion questions I get each week about
careers, loves, and destinies—which to me, from here,
are kind of like . . . crayons.

E-w-w-h-h, nice magenta!

*Sure, use all the tools, guides, and helpers you like,
I approve of them, too, but maybe, reread the fourth paragraph above as well.*

Do you remember way back when,

on the day you first earned your wings, how you worried about whether or not you'd be able to use them to lift yourself, and thereby the entire planet, higher?

And so I reminded you that the reason you earned them was because you already had?

You've already earned all that your heart desires.

Besides, you didn't really think with all the encrusted diamonds, inlaid pearls, and the monogrammed gold flaps you special-ordered, they were really about flying even higher, did you? I don't even know how you walk around with them things. But I'm proud as can be.

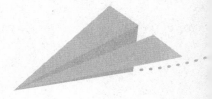

Of course it's true

everyone's born with a gift. One that will allow them to fill a
special place in the Universe that absolutely no one else can fill.
A blessing that makes all other blessings pale in comparison.
A gift of incalculable value to the entire world when it's
uncovered, explored, and embraced.

Yours?

Being you.

WOW, you must have known someone really "high up!"

Happiness isn't a crop
that you harvest when your dreams come true.

It's more like the fertilizer that makes them come true, faster.

Go ahead, want it all.
Just learn to be happy before it arrives,
or you may not notice when it does.

Hurry! It won't be long!

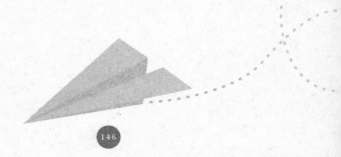

The adulation. The worship.
The glory. The throngs. The masses. The fans.

You'd think by now the novelty would have worn off—
but those few (and I do mean few, by our standards) who are
brave enough to adventure into the jungles of time and space
have our deepest admiration.

Because even though we know that wherever they find themselves,
nothing will be as it seems; that no matter what happens,
they'll always be safe and protected; and that their inevitable
homecoming celebration will make the Academy Awards look like
a McDonald's Happy Meal, they know none of this. And so the
heights of their glory and the depths of their despair have become
legend in a land of legends.

And you thought "reality TV" was popular?
You should see your ratings!

If you ever find yourself driving
down the motorway of life looking for an exit that says EASY
STREET, may I remind you that that's where you got on, following
a sign that said PARADISE, THIS WAY. ROAD UNDER CONSTRUCTION.
WATCH OUT FOR "LIGHT WORKERS," FALLING DEBRIS, POTHOLES, AND
SLIPPERY PATCHES. NO TURNING BACK.

And you said, "Cool."

What do you mean, "Are we there yet?"
You're now one of the light workers.

Now! Go! Stake your claim!

Hold out your hands. Move, get ready, give thanks.
Imagine, and let go. Act, and have faith. Persist.
Do what you can, when you can, all you can.

Because never again, not in a million years, not over
ten thousand lifetimes, will you ever again be as
close as you are today.

Ungawwa,
The Universe

From an endless sea

of wistful souls who've waited out eternity, it's now your turn,
in time and space. And there are simply no words that can express
just how uniquely special this privilege is.

Nor how fleeting.

Rising suns and babbling brooks.

Tropical forests and sleeping meadows. Modern marvels and scientific breakthroughs. Exciting discoveries and limitless frontiers. Devoted friends and caring strangers. Lives and loves and souls to hold so close, one's own heart could burst.

Look at it like this: it's not so much that you *have to* wait for your dreams to come true, but that you *get to*— in a Garden of Eden, the paradise of paradises, in the palm of my hand.

Can you even count the splendors?

Here's a little "Inevitability Test"

to check on the progress you're making toward
achieving any particular dream.

You're pretty much doing something about it,
every single day.

Yes, visualizing counts.
But preparing the way counts twice.
And acting "as if" it's a done deal, seven times.

You're thanking me?!

No. Sorry. I'm afraid you were misinformed.
You see, it's me who thanks you, every moment of
every day, for all that you are.

You have no idea.

Thank you, thank you, thank you.

Waiting for your life to take off?

That could be the problem.

Of all the luck!

Can you believe it?
You. In paradise. Now. Exactly as you are.
Exactly as it is.

Do you have any idea how many souls in the unseen wish they could be in your shoes? Wish they could see through your eyes? Wish they could feel what moves in your heart? Have your friends? Share your loves? Face your fears and your beasts?

Oh, heck yeah, your fears and your beasts! Are you kidding? Especially your fears and your beasts! Because from where they are, it's so much easier to see how soon they will pass, how triumphant you will be, and how much more they'll make possible.

To them, it's like every day is your birthday.

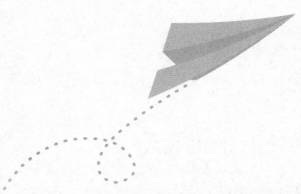

Haven't you always found your way?

Hasn't there always been a light in the darkness? Haven't you always gotten back up? Haven't there always been serendipitous surprises, unexpected twists, and triumphant comebacks? And haven't you always had someone to love?

Not to mention all of your dreams that have already come true.

Coincidences?

Or maybe, do you think, you, too, have always been loved?

Today there are "likelihoods,"

no concretes, no absolutes, nothing predestined or set in stone,
just "likelihoods."

And the ones that will come to pass *will all pivot*
on you and your thoughts.

You're *that* powerful.

Ever stop to realize

that it's impossible to feel true unconditional love for any single
person, until you can feel it for every single person?

After all, what differentiates them, except conditions?

Of course, it doesn't hurt to try.

Yes, even the clods.

What a cool month.

What a cool day.

Thoughts, still manifesting as predictably as the tides rise.

You, still as free to choose those thoughts, as the wind blows.

Seems all is well in paradise.

Anything else I can do for you, anything at all?

Love,

The Universe

Yeah, right. Sorry. As if something could beat the power to have it all.

Guess I'm just in one of those silly moods. XXOO

Never forget,

the scorecard that matters most is invisible, and won't be seen by
others until the game is over. At which point it'll be distributed
via our version of high-def broadband, in 5-D Technicolor,
to everyone you've ever known, and then some.

Of course, all the check boxes will be blank, except for where
you might want to rate yourself (highly discouraged, by the
way), but still, every single fear you ever faced, every bridge you
ever crossed, and every life you ever touched will be known and
celebrated by all.

*Actually, the party's already started, but it gets a little bigger every day as the ripples
created by your kindness and courage spread farther and farther.
Hey, you're HUGE in the unseen.*

Now, let's just say

you're a fisher person, and let's just say that I've rearranged
the stars so that this is going to be the luckiest week of your life.

Whoohooo!

Tell me, next time you go out on your boat,
will you take one pole, or many? Many. I thought so.

Would you think, maybe for the glimmering of a moment, that as
a lucky person, you won't have to fish anymore, because the fish
will come to you? No. Probably not. You've always been one of
the sharper tools in the shed.

So tell me, why is it so easy for most to see that with luck, even, they still have to put themselves out there, and that the more they do, the greater the yield. Yet when it comes to life's magic, thoughts becoming things, and the elements conspiring on their behalf, they think their fish will come to them?

Your first mate, always,
The Universe

No, there's no such thing as luck. Just folks who believe in the magic enough to "fish" at every opportunity.

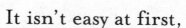

It isn't easy at first,

but one of the greatest gifts you could ever give someone who
makes your heart soar is the freedom to learn their own lessons,
at their own pace.

Even trickier is discovering that one of the greatest gifts you could
ever give someone who gets on your nerves is the freedom to
learn their own lessons, at their own pace.

And perhaps most challenging of all is understanding that one
of the greatest gifts you could ever give *yourself* is understanding
that your heart soaring and your nerves fraying have never been
dependent upon other people and their lessons.

In all cases, I meant, "besides chocolate."

Have you noticed it, too?
How fears are a lot like highway billboards?

The faster you're moving, the quicker they approach, the larger they get, and the more they block your view of what's real and alive. To the point that they tower above you, larger than life itself, giving you pause and more reason than ever to turn around and retreat to safety.

Yet if you muster the courage to stay the course, in just a blink they're behind you, put into proper perspective. And then as quickly as they appeared, they completely vanish.

If you want to stay the course, then please, just stay the course.

That's why we did away with billboards here a long time ago.
Besides, no one uses our highways.

It's easy.
Really easy.
All of it.

It's all *really* easy.

Yikes! I'm freakin'!
The holidays aren't far off and I have no idea what
to get for eight billion people this year!

Do you have any idea how difficult it is shopping for
folks who already have dominion over all things?

There's nothing I can give them that they can't give themselves.

Pretend you were me.

You're about to create a new reality. And you know you're
gonna hang out there, in every imaginable form, for
trillions and trillions and trillions of years.

Do you think, just for yucks, you'd build it in such a way that you
might get hurt, become less, or not matter?

Or, as the Universe, the alpha and the omega, the bringer of the
dawn and each new day, would you be pretty confident that you
could craft the most spectacular paradise imaginable? Flawless in
every way, yet possessing the odd illusions of pain, loss, and your
own irrelevance to heighten suspense, enhance the unknown,
and make it one unforgettable, spine-tingling, nonstop
adventure that will mean even more to you when you master it
again, but from the inside out?

CUT! That's a wrap.

Nice alpha! Were the purple leotards your idea?

XXOO,
The Universe

Don't believe the illusions.

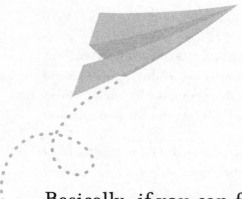

Basically, if you can feel it,
I can deal it.

Whatever you want.

With compliments,
The Universe

*Emotion summons circumstances. The greater the emotion,
the greater the circumstances.*

"Roger!" You have been heard.

And at this very moment, every single atom in the cosmos
is being reprogrammed, every single angel is being
summoned, and big wheels are a-turning.

We just hope you weren't kidding.

You're always heard. Every single thought.

To clear up a little something:

When it comes to your every cup overflowing...

Yes, I thought you'd remember that one.

Well, we neglected to add it's a self-service "bar."

But isn't that better than having to ask, wait, and hope?

Ever wonder

what the world would be like without you?

Who would shine a light into all the dark corners
you now illuminate? Who would comfort, guide,
and inspire all those you now reach? Who would
smile to those who need your smile the most?

We do.
All the time.
And it ain't pretty.

Oh, dearie, dearie me . . .

So many claim to believe.

So here's what I'm going to start asking them:
If you really believed you were guided, wouldn't
you begin listening?

And if you really believed you were powerful, wouldn't every
true desire be followed by action? And if you really believed
you could provide the spark that makes your dreams come true,
wouldn't you stop living as if you weren't sure?

That ought to stir up their coffee, huh?

Let's rock-and-roll.

Be the miracle.

You might not readily believe

this, it might even spook you a bit, but there are those (actually, far more than you could ever guess) who chose this very lifetime, in large part, knowing you'd be there.

Now, that's what we call a reputation.

Everyone's kind

to people they like.

Big whoop-dee-do!

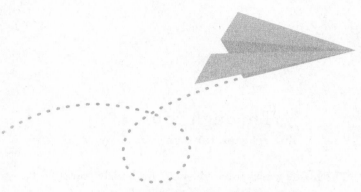

Here's a little trick
to get the ball rolling.

Ask yourself, "What's the most fun I could have with my life,
as it is now, before those big dreams of mine come true?"

Then, do it. A lot.

The next thing you know, those big dreams will come true.

*And, if you're not even sure what's fun anymore, then just do
anything. A lot. And it will find you.*

Through you,
through you, through you...

The magic works through you. Not beside you.
Not around you. Not for you. Not despite you.
But through you.

You have to go there. You have to choose your stage.
You have to do your dance. Putting yourself in place, to any
degree that you can, even if it scares you, even when it's "hard,"
even if it's just your big toe. Stretch yourself, scoff at the odds,
get the ball rolling so that the magic can then come alive and
sweep you off your feet with its infinite grace and glory.

You wouldn't just carry around the seeds for the garden of your
dreams in your pocket, all the while asking where your flowers
are? Nope, you'd have to brave the elements, you'd have to
choose the location, and then you'd have to go there.

Tally-hoe,
The Universe

When it comes to others,

rather than wishing they were somehow different, it's better to
give thanks that they are exactly as they are, because truly,
if they weren't, they wouldn't even be in your life right now.

Just wanted to let you know

that everyone here is rooting for you.

There will always be something

else you could have said. There will always be something else
you could have done. And there will always be
another life you could have lived.

But, frankly, we're still savoring all you did say, do, and become,
in spite of so many reasons that you might not have.

*Yeah, "What would [insert your name here] do?" is part of our pop vernacular
now. And you should see your pending endorsement deals . . . Magic carpets,
body wands, pixie dust, the works!*

It's that simple.

Your thoughts do become things. Don't resist it. Don't think
there's something else. Don't entertain the false premises of fate,
luck, or a God who judges, withholds, or decides. You decide.
You manifest. You rule. This is why you're here. This is what you
came to discover. To experience your absolute dominion over
every flimsy, malleable illusion of time and space.
To do, be, and have.

Truthfully, it couldn't be any easier. Not any.

All you have to do is think of what you want, and not deviate from
that thought. Which will invariably set you in motion, stir up the
magic, and unleash the full force, power, and majesty
of a Universe conspiring on your behalf.

Just do it. It's worth everything you've got.

Be strong, vigilant, and determined, and the
Kingdom of Heaven will appear at your very feet.

I got your back.

Imagine . . .

You're sitting upon your throne overlooking your Kingdom
(Queendom, whatever 'dom you like), and masses upon
masses of people surround you in throngs.

They're cheering your name, laying flowers at your feet, and
imploring you to join them in the village where they've
prepared a feast to celebrate your life.

You humbly accept their invitation, and immediately you're
whisked off your feet and lifted high upon the shoulders of your
joyful admirers, thoroughly overwhelmed by their heartfelt
gratitude and desire to please you.

Midway through the most extravagant party you've ever attended,
amid laughter and happy tears, you begin reflecting on your life
and in no way can you recall what you've done to deserve
such an outpouring of love.

Suddenly embarrassed, and wondering if you aren't dreaming
the whole thing, you turn to a member of your entourage and
whisper in her ear, "Are you sure there hasn't been some kind of
mistake? I mean, I don't even recall having a Kingdom!
Who are all these people? Who do they think I am?"

And she whispers back, "There's no mistake.
They know exactly who you are. These are just some of the souls
whose lives had reached a fork in the road, as most lives do,
where hope and despair had met, and because of something you
said or did—directly or indirectly—they were, as you might say,
shown the way, reborn, and, eventually, able to shine their light
onto the paths of *others* in need. That's who they are, and in case
you haven't noticed, more keep arriving in a procession
that will never end.

"And no, this isn't a dream."

And no, again. I didn't say "thongs." But I'd imagine that could be arranged.

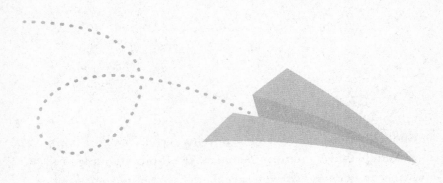

Do you know what you've created?

No, besides an intergallactically known saunter named after you.

Inspiration, in the eyes that have watched you.
Hope, in the minds that have admired you.
And love, in the hearts that have known you.

Not bad, kiddo, not bad at all.

But you might ease up on your sashay before someone gets hurt.

Here's some advice

for those who come to you with long faces.

"If you've finally decided, once and for all, to be happy, yet you aren't . . . then you haven't yet decided to be happy, once and for all."

Same goes for all the other stuff they've decided.

They're that powerful.

Always being your best, shining your brightest, and standing as tall as you can pays far more dividends than one might ever imagine.

Always take the high road.
And I'll see you there.

Contrary to popular thinking,
being worthy isn't something you earn, it's something you
recognize. And once you do, you won't be able to think, speak,
or behave in any other way than as if what you most wanted, was
meant to be. And so it shall be, because truly there's no one
worthier than you.

Don't you marvel at nature?

I do, but then I'm partial. It holds so many clues about living the life of your dreams, don't you think?

For instance, have you ever seen a mama duck waiting around for her ducklings to line up before crossing the street?

Never. Because she knows that the only way her ducklings are ever going to line up is if she first starts out on a new adventure.

Just one of your ducks,
The Universe

It's the same for your ducks, they won't line up, either, until you start.

New Soul Orientation

The following words and phrases are not in my vocabulary:
"Should." "Difficult." "Evil." "I don't know."

Oh sure, there'll be plenty of times you can use them, and
everyone will know exactly what you mean—especially me—at which
point all the elements will conspire to make them true for you.

I also never ask, "How?" Might as well just ask, "What Universe?"

Dismissed,
This Universe

Oh, and there's one more. "Good-bye." It's a bit of fiction that totally tears me up.

Friends and partners

to celebrate life with, abundance to enhance any adventure,
and mountains to perch atop, all arrive when you dwell upon
the celebration, the adventure, and the view. Not the names,
lotteries, or path you think wisest.

This is so important—because I want you to have them all.

Yes, you can have whatever you want, anything. Just please don't confuse what you want with how you're going to get it.

"Reality" is not that you are weak,

and dream of becoming strong.

Poor, and dream of becoming rich.

Alone, and dream of having friends.

But that you're already strong, rich, and among friends;
yet, at times, dream that you're not.

Sometimes the suspense
here becomes almost too much.

Like right now.

Before you, in the unseen, there are some amazing,
mind-blowing circumstances now brewing. Wheels are turning,
fires are burning, and all possibilities are being recalculated.
Players, player-ettes, and accomplices are lining up,
soon to burst into your life.

All just waiting for the nod from me . . .
as I wait for the nod from you.

Wha-Hu-Ha! This is so much fun!

Once you know, commit and never look back.

Best friends may tell you

what to do. Yep, because that's what best friends do.

Wise friends, however, wouldn't dream of it because they
understand that they'll never know of all the secrets that stir
in your heart, of your gifts that lie in waiting, or of the
plans that we have made.

S-h-h-h-h-h,
The Universe

And I'm not telling.

Thinking big but acting small,
is the same as thinking small.

Shiver me timbers.

Reading this and nodding in wholehearted agreement,
but not doing a little acting "as if your dreams have come true"
in the days that follow, is the same as not reading this.

I'm everywhere . . .
Between the bombs, beside each soldier, and in the racing hearts
of every combatant, I now reside joyfully radiant. Knowing that
an unfolding war, like all catastrophes, will ultimately serve to
awaken your spirit, draw you together, and inspire an everlasting
compassion as you begin to finally realize that the glint in your
enemy's eye . . . was only a tear.

One hundred trillion years!
7 continents!
113 billion people! (not counting Atlantis, and the others)
96 zillion dreams manifested!

And not once, not even close, not even on my most generous, loving, caring days, has anything ever happened in time and space—good or bad, big or small, rich or poor—that wasn't sparked by someone's imagination and followed up with their own baby steps.

Now remind me, what is it you most want?

Not without you,
The Universe

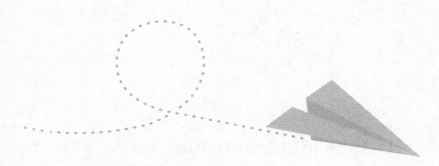

Pssst . . . Hey, gorgeous!
Want to know a secret?

Everything in your life is a symbol. A reflection. A clue.
A reminder. Of what you understand, and of what you don't,
made manifest.

Look to the beauty for truth. And to what hurts, for its beauty.

*Oh, yes indeed, life is fair. As fair as it is beautiful. Though this can't always be seen
from too close, in terms of either time or space.*

When life hurts.

When it baffles and confuses. When it doesn't quite seem to
work. These are just signs from Me, as if I were tapping on your
shoulder or whispering in your ear, trying to point out that
something important, something really, really important,
is being misunderstood.

Actually, while it's fun

to think about how fantastically different life will be once
your ship comes in, the truth is, the only thing that will really
change, is you.

Hey, why wait?

If you knew of a spectacular mountain

that was very, very tall, yet climbable, and if it was well established
that from its peak you could literally see all the love that bathes
the world, dance with the angels, and party with the "Gods,"
would you curse, or celebrate, each step you took
as you ascended it?

Right-o. Life is that mountain, and each day a step.

Have no fear.
Last time I checked, you were so close to the top
they were taking your toga measurements.

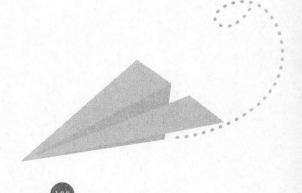

Ever pour cement?

Heavy stuff, but it's a simple job. Just mix, set, and leave it alone. You can even make shapes out of it, like ducks, flowers, or figurines, depending on the mold. There's no limit.

Now, let's just say that you don't like the way a particular duck came out. Would you try to repour or manipulate the cast concrete, or would you simply start over, considering that cement is dirt cheap?

Oh, you're way ahead of me! You saw that "mix, set, and leave" was like a metaphor for using your imagination, didn't you? You also got that the mold is your goal or dream. I think the "no limit" tipped you off, too. "Heavy stuff," "simple," and "cheap" were also clues. But what I'm most proud of is that you saw how repouring or manipulating cast concrete is like trying to effect change in one's life by tweaking what's already manifested, instead of going within and manifesting anew.

Five Gold Stars for you today,
The Universe

What if,

when you lay your head upon your pillow tonight, you could
choose to slip into a dream dimension where time would literally
expand, so much so that you could live out an entire other
lifetime within it as a person "designed" by you from head to toe,
even choosing your name and who your parents would be?

Where every single day you'd be pushed on to greatness, every
single challenge would invite you to become more, and all of your
dreams could come true?

Where, no matter how things may ever seem, you'd be bathed
in love, surrounded by friends, safe and sound
in your very own bed?

And where, upon waking, all that you loved and learned in
that lifetime would remain with you, and all that scared and
threatened you would only have prepared you for even more love
and learning in the near future?

And what if it were possible, for the most adventurous and enquiring minds, to actually wake up within that dream, to really light things up, manifest some bling, and heal the odd fellow adventurer?

"Odd" in a good way.

Would you choose to go there, just for one night, on the condition that during the dream itself you mustn't have any recollection of how you got there, its purpose, or what might happen next?

Howling at the moon,
The Universe

PS—How's it going?

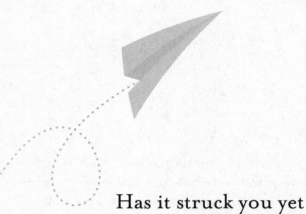

Has it struck you yet

that answers come before questions?

That healing begins with illness?

And that you can't have a dream come true
without a time when it hasn't?

Shoot, isn't it all so perfect? Everyone, no matter where they are
on their journey, can be happy.

At all times, and in all matters, everything is happening in your favor.

Please, don't be afraid.
Not even a little. Not ever.

The lions and tigers and bears can't really hurt you. You live in a world of fog and mirrors where there's only the illusion that you could somehow become less than the greatest you've ever imagined yourself to be. And it's this very image, the highest from within you, that has summoned your boldest dreams, daring you into the light with their sweet rewards and drawing you through the very fears that have kept you from it.

Slayer of dragons. Matador of all time and space. Rightful heir to heaven on earth. Don't be afraid. Not even a little.

Amen,
The Universe

I guess I just needed to blog.

There are lots of people
out there whose lives would be made "richer,"
if only they'd "let you in."

And perhaps, vice versa?

The thing to remember,
to always remember, is that what you do,
or don't do, today, is what matters most.

In fact, nothing else does.

Imagine yourself

on a warm summer evening before a calm, clear pond. The moon
is full. The stars are shining. Whippoorwills are
whippoor-willing. And I am with you.

Now, do you know how to float on water? For the most part
you do absolutely nothing, at which point I can hold you at the
surface, in the palm of my hand. It's simply a matter of physics,
the laws of time and space, and your natural state.

Are you with me?

Okay, now you'll have to trust me, but it's the same when it
comes to floating in wealth and abundance, health and harmony,
friends and laughter. These are your natural state, your default
settings, the "givens" in this great adventure. These are where
true balance is found. They can be yours without strenuous
effort. You don't even have to visualize them. Just stop the
argument that claims you're without. Surrender in the war that
presumes lack. Come out from the fort that has kept you so safe,
and follow your heart with abandon.

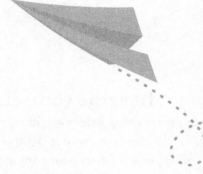

It's as if,

when moving from point A to point B in your life—from sickness to health, poverty to wealth, whatever—at some point in the journey, arriving at point B becomes inevitable, a sure thing. However, at no point in your journey is this physically verifiable—until you reach point B.

The point being (yuck, yuck), you may have already crossed that line. But you'll never know it, unless you see the journey through.

Without a doubt,

right here and now, as you read these very words with eyes that sparkle, this golden day, amid your dancing manifestations in a perfect world on an emerald planet while your heart beats, your blood flows, and angels peer over your shoulder, I think you just might be the luckiest person alive.

The best way to find "love,"

which, incidentally, is just as true for finding money, is to focus less on these by-products of a life well lived and more on a life well lived.

Simple is as simple does.

Dance life's dance, today, without preconditions.

Time and space, what a hoot.

Look to them for answers, direction, and meaning,
and they'll rock your world every which way.

Yet discover that they look to *you* for answers, direction,
and meaning, and *you* will rock the world.

Take my word for it, the latter is your "ticket."

Tallyho, maestro—
The Universe

What an adventure, if I do say so myself.

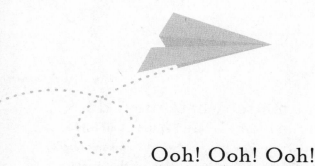

Ooh! Ooh! Ooh!

Have I mentioned that everyone knows exactly
what you're thinking?

How else could you draw new friends from the unseen? How
else would your heroes, heroines, and scoundrels know when to
appear, or move on? How else would your "stars" get their cues?

True, they think their own thoughts, too. How else would you
know who to cast in each scene?

Just thinking of you, and your power to choose.

Yes . . . even those thoughts!

It doesn't matter what "they" do.

Your net worth, net health, and net happiness all hinge
exclusively upon your net thoughts, net words, and net deeds.
Though little can rob you as quickly as thinking that it matters
what "they" do.

You've got the power.

Perhaps the most exciting realization

in the world is finally understanding that living the
life of your dreams is entirely up to you.

It's also about the scariest.

Until you realize that "you" includes "Me."

If it was just about surviving,

getting by, and keeping things the way they are, then how
would you explain imagination?

If it was just about sacrifice, selflessness, and altruism,
then how would you explain desire?

And if it was just about thinking, reflecting, and spiritual stuff,
then how would you explain the physical world?

Vroom, vroom,
The Universe

Want it all. That's what it, and you, are there for.

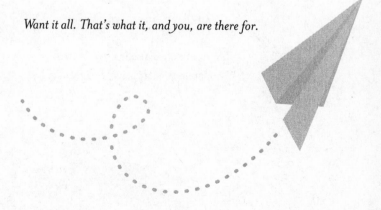

You could call me your friend,

but that's not quite enough. You could call me your guide, but there's more to it than that.

You could call me your conspirator, your helper, or your agent; your coach, counselor, or confidant; your father, mother, or child. You could call me the sun, the moon, and the stars; the wind, the sky, and the rain; the past, the present, and the future.

But really, what I'm getting at, the purpose behind all these Notes, and perhaps what I'd most like to hear one day, is you calling me "yourself."

O-h-m-m-m-m-m...

Just as I've always called you "myself."
(With unimaginable pride, I might add.)

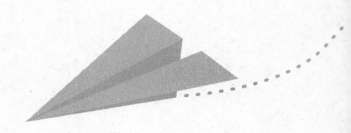

Getting what you think about,

being loved and adored, and having the whole world spin in the
palm of your hand aren't things you learn, earn, or force.

Breathing is enough.

Because you already do, you already are, and it already does.

Fear just means

you've forgotten how deeply you're loved,
how safe you are, and that happiness will return,
like you've never known it before.

It doesn't change these things.

Of course you sometimes feel

alone, confused, and frightened! You come from an ancient spiritual family of the finest imaginable lineage, loved and respected by all. They threw the happiest parties, knew the happiest souls, and lived in mansions of solid gold. They were so adored and respected throughout the cosmos that whatever they wanted, they received twelve times over.

You, however . . .

Wel-l-l-l, it's like when it came time for your education and the furthering of your divine awareness, you just had to go far, far away. To the most remote little school ever heard of, deep within the jungles of time and space, called Earth. Created quite the stir, you did. Until, of course, you began sending home postcards from the sleep state. Now, as you might have guessed, they toast your name every single night in total awe of your courage.

Me, too.

You hooligan.

I have to tell you

that one of the greatest things about being the Universe is knowing
absolutely everything.

Well, that, and making dreams come true.

I also love being eternal. And having no limits.

Creating worlds simply with thought.

Knowing that reality is unfolding just exactly as it should.

Having it all, being it all, doing it all.

And I like being perpetually in love, and loved.

How 'bout you?

What's your favorite thing about
being the Universe?

xxxxxxxxxxxxxxx ooooooooooooooooooo!

S-h-h-h-h-h-h-h!
Don't say a word and off with the lights!

Now is as good a time as any to watch *It's a Wonderful Life*.
No, no, not the one with Jimmy Stewart! The other one!
You know . . . starring you. It's the best. A total-underdog,
goose-bump, come-from-behind kind of adventure.
And what an "ending"!

Whooo-hoooo!

I especially love the part where you, in spite of all evidence to the
contrary, finally declare "enough is enough" (actually, far more
colorful language is used because we don't have a rating system
here) and you begin visualizing, putting up dream photos on
the computer, refrigerator, and mirrors, and start performing
simple acts of faith, as if your dreams had already come
true, every single bloomin' day.

The transformation that follows really pushes the envelope on believability. Except, of course, it's a true story!

It's also a great psych-up "watch" for new souls. You know, before their first big plunge.

Definitely two thumbs-up.

Shhhh . . . The best part is just now starting. You're about to do all that you can do, with what you've got, from where you are, and then turn it over to . . . the Universe! (My second-favorite character.)

Now, as the Universe

I don't like telling anyone what they should or shouldn't do.
But when the urge arises, I proceed in the most delicate,
gentle, and loving way possible:

You look radiant this morning! Did you enjoy our dreams last
night concerning the changes and manifestations you want?
Have you had a chance to paint a lovely picture in your mind of
the "end result"? Ready to move toward what you want, however
you can, whenever you can? Will faith and expectation be part
of your daily constitution? These things are really quite important,
you know. Actually, to effect any kind of change at all, honey...
don't even think there might be another way.

xxoo,
The Universe

There are some things, dearest, only you can do.

You do know what

they're going to do, don't you? And you do know
what they're going to say?

Yeah, once you consistently spend some time visualizing every
day, doing the "all you can with what you've got" dance, and
pushing yourself to live the life of your dreams to any degree that
you now can, so that the floodgates fly open and you have your
dream home, your dream work, and your dream friends?

They're gonna give you that long, cold glance out of the corner
of their eyes and say in a low, drawn-out voice, just loud
enough for you to hear, "Must...be...nice..."

Just warning you,
The Universe

*And you'll pause, look at them sympathetically, and say,
"Oh, actually you get used to it."*

Nothing is ever lost

in this adventure of all adventures. The lessons and discoveries of
every single life, no matter how large or small, difficult or easy,
are added to the whole. Like stones in the base of a pyramid,
they permanently raise, and forever support every manner
of adventure that follows. And so it is that the hearts of those
who came first continue to beat in all subsequent generations,
forevermore.

Every single life.

Worry?! Why?

Do you really think something could go "wrong"?
Are you not eternal? Have you forgotten how much you're loved?

Don't you see how far you've already come?

Could you possibly be in better hands?

Besides, your angels are so b–u–s–s–s–y right now . . .

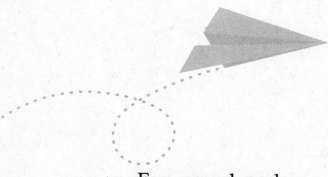

Ever wonder why

you sometimes feel like you're on top of your game? Ever wonder
why you sometimes feel so safe, secure, and deeply loved?

Ever wonder why there are days when you feel invincible,
unstoppable, and . . . well, like "King of the World"?

Actually, Your Highness, I often wonder why you don't
always have those feelings.

Impressed beyond belief,
The Universe

I loved that part in Titanic.

It's as if you're pounding

on the massive doors of the Kingdom of your Wildest Dreams. At first lightly, even respectfully. Then, losing patience, louder and louder.

You pray, you plead, you beg, you ask, you cry, you wail.

And just on the other side of the door, your faithful, adoring subjects silently writhe, some quietly crying, all intensely feeling your frustration and loneliness. Yet they remember all too well how on the day you left, you made them swear to not ever open the door so that you might discover, yourself. . .

that it was left unlocked.

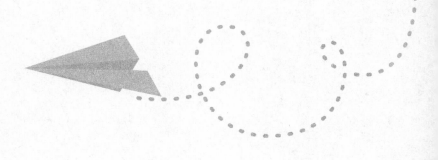

When you can't figure

out the hows, consider it a blessing, not a curse. Because you cannot imagine how much freer it makes you to simply dwell upon the end result, without fear, without doubt, and without worry. And really, that's what matters most.

You lucky salt.

It's not about what they did,

it's about what you'll do.

Worldwide Proclamation!

This is to remind all my loyal subjects that you are not my
loyal subjects. And that I'm bloody tired of all the sacrifices,
appeasements, and groveling.

I, the Universe—the sun, the moon, and the stars, the Alpha and
the Omega, and all the rest—have created a paradise in Time
and Space so that I, through you, might experience its infinite
splendors, drink from its every cup, and live, love, and be
merry in ways impossible without you.

Your desires are my desires for you. What you want and when you
want it, these were my ideas, too. Your dreams are my dreams.
You are the be-all and end-all of Time and Space, the only
reason for this Garden of Eden. You can do no wrong,
there are no mistakes, and it's all good.

Follow your heart, and delight in your preferences.
Approve of yourself. Stake your claim, demand it, and hold
out your hands. Banish your doubts, get off of your knees,
and live as you please. Because, dearest, you can,
and this is all I ever wanted.

With unspeakable love, I am,
The Universe

PS—ROAAAAAAAAAAAAAR!

For whatsoever you do
to further your dreams, I will do more.

How can you know
that something hasn't worked out, unless you quit?

Ah-so,
The Universe

*It is working out, you are getting closer,
it is getting easier, and . . . you're looking absolutely fantastic these days!*

So I was talking with this tree

awhile back. "Universe . . ." it said to me.

"Yeah?"

"When I come back, I don't want to be just wood."

"Well," I thought aloud, "what's wrong with being wood?"

"It's hard," the tree said, without cracking a smile. "When I come back, I want to be soft and furry so that I'll be loved by children."

And I thought . . . and thought . . . and thought . . . and finally asked, "Why not be tall and strong, just as you are, and loved by children?"

And the children came to play.

Do you really think you have to change to have what you want?

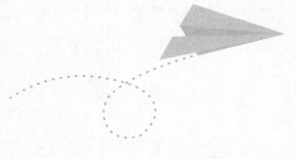

Remember that day

not so long ago, just before you took your first big gulp of air?

Sure, you remember . . . You were just a wispy thought and you vowed with clenched teeth and tight fists (figuratively), "This time I won't forget! This time I'll remember! This time, no matter how easy or difficult life gets, I'll refuse to look to the world around me for meaning, direction, or to invoke change, knowing instead that the world around me will only mirror all that moves within my heart and mind.

"This time, for meaning, direction, or to invoke change, I'll go within. All things are possible. Hip-hop, Scooby-Doo!"

Kind of odd, but you said it.

Oh, yes you did, who else talks like that?

I do not.

Kind of makes you wonder what happened last time, doesn't it?

There's no one in your life
who hasn't always loved you.

They're all just learning how to show it.

Like you.

It's simply a matter of applying
what you have to what you face. That's all that matters.

Because by design, what you have is always the greater.

Proudly yours,
The Universe

It hasn't always been this easy
being the Universe.

Before you came along, I was a lot less. Before you came along, there was no one who ever thought like you now think.

No one who ever felt what you now feel. And perhaps what I treasure most, no one who's ever possessed your priceless view of reality as you now perceive it. And all of these things who have been added unto me.

Thank you, you've done enough. You are enough. I am so pleased, you have no idea.

With love and adoration,
The Universe

Of course, my job would be easier still if you could see what I see—in you. This week, let's look together.

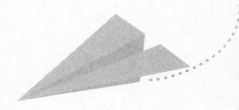

Perception Management
for Very Advanced Souls

The next time someone upsets you, think, "Thanks for
pointing out that I've begun depending on you. Time I lose the
expectations."

And the next time someone doesn't take your view into account,
think, "That's okay, I was once like that."

And if someone steals from you, think, "It was nothing, my
supply is the Universe." Or lies to you, think, "I'm sorry you
feel that need." Violates you, "All for my growth and glory."
Is rude to you, "Cheer up, dear soul, it'll be okay." Judges
you... "Thanks for sharing your truth." Drives by you like a "bat
out of hell"... "Be careful, my friend. I love you."

And the next time someone greets you with a smile,
smile back, like you're sharing a secret.

Oh, sure, there are other ways to deal with each scenario.
And Very Advanced Souls know that they're all okay.

Okay, let's try this . . .

Ever stop and realize that if there was no such thing as time and space, your thoughts would instantaneously manifest before you?

Thought so. Very good. You understand that in such a reality, there'd be no lag or delay as I jockeyed the players, events, and circumstances of your life into place.

Now, in such a reality, it would also be pretty easy to see that there'd be no outside, non-you factors, influencing, guiding, or directing the manifestations that occurred in your experience. Right? You'd simply choose your thoughts, and presto!

All right, then, if you suddenly added the parameters of time and space to this reality, can you still see that there wouldn't be any outside, non-you factors, influencing, guiding, or directing the manifestations that occur all around you? That if there were, you wouldn't have dominion over all things? Can you see, that under no circumstances would anything, ever, be predestined or "meant to be"? Not relationships, not jobs, not nothin'?

Further, can you see that any such hypothetical predetermined destinies would severely limit your ability to create your own reality, stifle your creativity, and make "null and void" the inviolate, universal principle of "thoughts become things"?

Excellent! Because that brings us to today and the morals behind this lesson:

1. Absolutely anything can happen in time and space, if you dream it up first.
2. Positively nothing will happen in time and space, if you don't.
3. Lags and delays should never be cause to assume something isn't meant to be. They're just the cloaks and curtains I work behind.

And, dearest, if you could see what I now see moving behind your curtains, you'd never, ever settle for less than exactly what you most want.

Yes! Yes! Yes!

Oh-h-h-h-h-h, y-e-s-s-s-s-s-s-s!

No. No. No. Not what you're thinking!
(But glad you're coming out of your shell.)

Just answering every single one of the requests I receive.
And the "Ohhhhhh, yesssssss!" was for the chap who didn't ask,
but who gave thanks in advance.

This may be hard to believe, but I never say no.

Whatever you want,
The Universe

PS—The "No. No. No," doesn't count.

Do you have any idea how many times a day I say, "Yes!" when the request is clear?
Actually, there isn't a number big enough to give you the slightest idea.

The novice learns to be honest

with others, in terms of who, what, when, and where.

The advanced soul learns to be honest with self, and discovers "perspective" rules, yet changes swiftly.

The Master, however, studies honesty in terms of motivation, where heretofore the lies have really piled up!

So . . . what do you really, really, really want, and why?

Being a Master can be a bear, huh?

I've made up my mind
about your dream job.

Yep, it's all yours.
Once you make up your mind.

Don't hate me.

Material Abundance
is simply spirit, celebrating.

*By the way, it's also the inevitable consequence
of enlightenment.*

(in-ev-i-ta-ble: impossible to avoid or prevent)

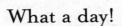

What a day!
I feel so great, so magnanimous, so everywhere!

Tell you what, today . . . dreams are on me.

Today everyone's dreams will come true!

Can I do that? Gimme a break.
I do it every single day, for everyone, everywhere,
no matter what. Always, second to second, month to month,
year to year, I give you what you think about, what you
most expect, what you believe in and move toward.

What else are Universes for?

And soon we shall see, literally, the thoughts you choose today.

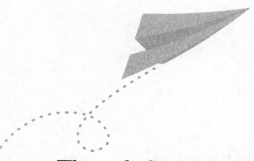

Those feelings you most want

aren't going to come from somewhere new, someone special,
or something wonderful.

Doesn't work like that.

They're going to come from within, where they
now wait for permission to be released—often in terms
of somewhere new, someone special,
or something wonderful.

Chic-a-boom,
The Universe

Whatever you hope to feel in the future, you can decide to feel right now.

Fret not.

Time is on your side.
So are *all* the angels.
And "no" is never forever.

Avoid gray areas.

There, the illusion of safety is guarded by the lies of "maybe,"
"sometimes," and "I don't know."

There is a truth. There is a way. Life is absolute, and its
principles exacting. If you put it out "there," it has to come back.
Ask, and it must be revealed.

Think, speak, and move with your desires,
and *nothing* will ever be the same.

Do you think gravity

has to work twice as hard to hold an elephant to the ground
as it does an acorn?

Ha.

So please understand, it's the same with the principle of
"thoughts become things." The size of your dreams has nothing
to do with the likelihood of them coming to pass, nothing.

Think BIG.

It's a matter of switching gears,

never looking back, and being the person today that
you've always dreamed you'd be.

Entertain every thought, say every word, and make every decision
from their point of view. Walk the way they would walk, dress
the way they would dress, and spend your free time the way they
would spend theirs. Choose the friends they would choose, eat
the meals they would eat, and love and appreciate yourself the
way they would.

These steps must come in order for there to be change. There's
no other option, no other way. But . . . since that person is who
you really are, that makes this assignment downright effortless.
Just stop being who you aren't.

Love,
The Universe

A Paradoxical Perspective
from your friend, the Universe:

On earth it seems that most people fret, worry,
and lose sleep over some of the silliest things they've done.

But what's funny is that later on, from here, more often than
not, it's the things they didn't do that haunt them.

I'm not laughing, either.

If at first you don't succeed,
it only means you're getting closer.

You wanna know

what the single toughest thing about figuring out time and
space is? About finally making progress by leaps and bounds
with the life of your dreams? The one thing that would heal every
broken heart and vanquish every emotional pain? That would
clear the way for infinite abundance, perfect health,
and unlimited happiness?

Not relying on appearances.

Now, you wanna know the easiest and simplest way to lick 'em?

Stop relying on appearances.

Just stop it.

You can.

What if today

you could wipe the slate clean, start over, and write your
own ticket?

No. Wait. Let's change that. What if every day you could wipe the
slate clean, start over, and write your own ticket?

How many days would have to go by before you discovered that
your "slate" and your "ticket" have nothing to do with each other?
That your past need not live in your future?

Your absolute freedom and total power lie in the present moment.

Hoping, wishing, and praying
shouldn't ever be confused with doing.

Know what I mean?

As in, doing "all you can, with what you've got, from where you are."

Always, the best remedy
for dealing with a troubled past is living in the present.

Would you believe

that there are some people who actually think they can
change their life through "pretending it better?"

Yep! And we call them Masters.

In awe of you,
The Universe

Sure beats pretending nothing is happening. Ha!

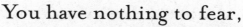

You have nothing to fear,

not even fear itself. Because in the final analysis,
you will find your way, you will be delivered,
and your every cup will overflow forever more.

This is set in stone.

Fear, fear, fear! People sure love to scare others
by telling them not to fear fear. Ha!

How'd you like a little peek

into the future? Oh, I really shouldn't, but, well,
you so rock, I figure this indulgence, just once, will be all right.

You're sitting around a warm and cozy fireplace surrounded
by friends and boisterous laughter. Early morning snow gently
falling across the countryside is visible from the enormous,
ceiling-high windows beside you. Everyone is sipping hot
chocolate and reminiscing about the fabulous circumstances that
have brought you together, brimming with excitement
for times ahead.

And then you chime in, "If only I'd seen it, I would never have been so hard on myself. If only I'd had just the slightest inkling that the challenges, lacks, and issues I faced back then were of my own exacting design, and that they'd soon make possible the whirlwind of events that so swiftly followed, I'd have been . . . well, as proud of myself back then as I am now."

And then your friends all start clapping.

Not a word to anyone.

You're also wearing the most outrageous sparkly tights I've ever seen. But then, you always could wear anything.

I'm soooooo excited!

Everything's just about ready.

I've arranged for all the right players to appear at all the right times. Big shots, little shots, and some absolute angels. (You aren't even going to believe who you'll soon be schmoozing with. Or where!)

I've lined up the necessary phone calls, emails, and chance encounters so that you'll be disposed to waves of loving, inspired thoughts precisely when most needed. I've calculated—literally to the billionth degree—the pivotal coincidences, happy accidents, and clutch plays that will blast you to heights previously unimagined. Even took care of "happily-ever-after."

So . . . how are things coming on your end?

And the day will come

when you will ask, "Whatever have I done to be so deserving of the
friends, laughter, and abundance that now surround me?"

And, of course, I will answer, "You rose to the challenge of seeing
yourself as divine and worthy, even while the rest of the world, at
first, saw you as neither. And you prevailed."

Well done, maestro. Well done, indeed.

The Universe

It's not the big dreams

I have trouble with, but the little ones.

Do us all a favor; think HUGE.

Think of everything, all of it.

Every mountain before you, every pound you carry, every dollar
you wish to manifest . . . as if it were made of pixie dust.

Suddenly—*dun, dun, dun, dunnnnnnn*—dominion
over all things isn't so intimidating, huh?

Like Beethoven?
You should hear his latest.

How quickly would you like

to be surrounded by wealth and abundance?
Have even more friends and enjoy more laughter?
How fast would you like to grow a thriving business,
or have your own fabulous house on the water?

If you answered "pronto," "ASAP," or "duh" to any or all
of these questions, could it be that you've momentarily
forgotten that the absolute fastest way to manifest change is to
claim that you already have it? To withdraw your attention from
the yearning? To think, speak, and act "as if"?

I didn't think so.

The very same magic,

the very same, that you used to get your first job, to find a
best friend, and to heal the hurt that even now finishes your
sentences, beats your heart, and inspires your dreams,
is the exact same "grade" of stuff that can make what you most
want today come to pass.

Point being: You've already engaged it. You've
already commanded it. You've already done the
bloody impossible!

So what's the big deal about doing it again?

Oh, go on . . .

In all my years as the Universe,
never once have I asked for anything in return of anyone,
anywhere, ever.

And I think that's a pretty good policy, no matter who I am.

Don't you?

Think less, feel more.

Those folks who find success,

and then tell the world it was due to their hard work, really make my job challenging.

They almost never work harder than others. They don't even work smarter than others. They simply engaged the magic by thinking, speaking, and acting in line with what they wanted.

But oh, no, they have to go out and tell impressionable minds that it was their hard work. And when those minds "buy it" the bar is raised for them.

Do yourself a favor, engage the magic.

To touch someone with kindness

is to change someone forever.

Wild, huh? That's nothing.

Because for everyone you touch, you also reach everyone they will ever know. And everyone they will ever know. And everyone they will ever know. And so, for the rest of all time, your kindness will be felt, in waves that will spread, long after you move on.

Muchas gracias,
The Universe

Don't ask what happens on a "bad" day.

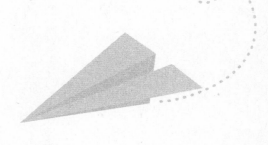

What are you doing about it?

*Because it takes you doing what you can do, before I can do
what I can do—you know, miracles and stuff.*

The trouble

with troublesome people is that they often
have much to teach those they trouble.

Love 'em all.

However do you do it?

You know, talk, and make such sense? Walk, and not fall down?
Ask, and then know the answer? Aim, and then deliver?
Show up on time? Always get by? Make just enough?

How on earth?!

You don't know how, do you? You haven't got a clue.

And that's exactly how you do it. You leave the details, the "hows,"
to Me—as you simply focus upon and move toward the end result.
Expectant, even.

Dreams come true the same way.

No matter what your faith is,

or is not. No matter where in the world you are.
I want you to know, I'll be with you. Behind the eyes of every
child, and in the melody of every song, I'll be the glimmer in the
ice crystals, the rays in the sun, and the stars at night.

And with each smile you see, every hug you receive, and every
laugh you hear, I'll be there reaching out through another,
with blessings and tidings to last you the year, because I love you.
Because I've always loved you. And because I always will.
And because this has been true, and will be true,
every day of your life.

Blessings to you, to your family, and to every single wonderful,
radiant Being in your shimmering, enlightened sphere.

Remember this, and be sure to look for me—all year long.

If you have to ask for "signs,"

let this need of yours be a "sign" that you should
make haste very s-l-o-w-l-y.

There are those

who absolutely think all the right thoughts.
Yet if they're not doing all they can, with what they've got,
from where they are, then you can just guess what else
they're probably thinking.

And those other thoughts are busy at work, too.

Let's just say

you're driving down the road listening to some hip-hop, happy kind of music. Then, after a while, you decide you want to hear something else, maybe some classic rock. Would you just hope that the hip-hop station starts playing rock? Would you visualize it, and say, "YES! I believe in the magic! I know that thoughts become things! I can 'see' the Boss now, I can 'hear' the E Street Band. Thank you, Universe, in advance, thank you, thank you, thank you. I am so grateful!"?

Or after thinking about what you wanted, would you change the station?

Good. Just checking.

Rock on,
The Universe

I don't quite know

if it's the way your mind works, or your emotional sensitivity.

I don't know if it's the way you laugh, or the way you cry.
Could be your tenacity and courage. Or maybe it's your wit and
spontaneity.

Truth is there's never been anyone like you,
so it's hard to tell. But whatever it is, to me, from here,
right now, you sure improve the view.

You are soooo beautiful.

Gratefully,
The Universe

There comes a time

in the evolution of every spiritual being, along that sometimes
dark road that leads to enlightenment, when their inner
yearnings, struggles, and frustrations bring them to a truth that
could not otherwise have been achieved. And so, dearly beloved,
I come this sacred day with such a truth, though it may
temporarily hurt eyes that have been shut too long.

Reaching this milestone was inevitable, for the light that will
dawn hereafter is not only what you have summoned, but what all
now seek. And with your blessing and recognition, it will bathe
those who follow in your footsteps and the burden they bear
shall be lessened.

A more perfect child of the Universe has never existed. Until
now, only a celebration cloaked in myth and mystery could hint at
your sublime heritage and divine destiny. You are life's prayer of
becoming, and its answer. The first light at the dawn of eternity,
drawn from the ether, so that the Universe might know its depths,
discover its heights, and frolic in endless seas of blessed emotion.

A pioneer into illusion, an adventurer into the unknown, and a lifter of veils. Courageous, heroic, and exalted by countless souls in the unseen.

To give beyond reason. To care beyond hope. To love without limit. To reach, stretch, and dream in spite of fear. These are the hallmarks of divinity—traits of the immortal— your badges of honor, and your ticket home.

This is the time of year we celebrate who you are.

The Universe

Hmmmm . . . Think I should switch to decaf?

You know how sometimes

when you visualize, you end up daydreaming, too?

Or when you finally remember to perform an act of faith,
it feels kind of hokey?

Or sometimes you catch yourself worrying, or thinking too much
about the past, or wondering whether or not you have invisible,
limiting beliefs holding you back?

Well, that's exactly what all Illuminates go through (especially the
good-looking ones). But they arrive in spite of it, and so will you.

Worry not; just keep chugging.

Hugs,
The Universe

No, not as in gulp, gulp, but as in choo, choo.

All right, you know how in golf,

when you play with a friend and they hit the ball really, really close to the cup, only a stroke away from sinking it, you say, "Great shot, that's a 'gimme'!" (Meaning you're not going to make them putt the next one, because they'd probably make it, so you just give it to them?) Just say, "Yes."

Right!

Well, about your dreams . . . The good news is that they're so close to manifesting that in golf they'd be "gimmes"!

Right again! This ain't golf . . . and it's your turn.

Whoa...
did you mean for this to be happening?

Did you intend to change the course of history?

Do you fully comprehend the "ripple effect"?

Well, just so you know, these are the unavoidable consequences of thoughtfulness, patience, and unbridled kindness.

I love it when you're wild and crazy.

Don't all those goody-goodies
who tell you that life is "how you take it" make you
want to scream?!

Me, too, but let's have patience with them.

Life's not about how you take it, it's about the glory of manifesting your own "luck" and crafting circumstances, magnetizing players and forging alliances, leveraging your wits and engaging the magic so that you can have the sun, the moon, and the stars. Full stop.

Okay, you're sitting

in a little room, staring out the only window you've ever known, at a world that's so incredibly beautiful you can hardly believe your good fortune. Every night you draw the blinds to sleep and every sunrise you rush to the window to gaze some more. Your life is idyllic.

Now, let's just say, one day while gazing out the window at the wondrous, lush, enchanting paradise you've come to love, something incredible happens. Bulldozers appear, workers descend, and construction begins on a huge, gigantic chicken statue that destroys your view.

Assuming you've never had a fondness for chicken statues, what would you do next?

A. Learn to love the chicken statue, since it is "of God," too?
B. Live off the memory of what used to be?
C. Call a lawyer and begin litigation?
D. Pick up your chair and move to another little room with a totally different view, in your incredible, magical mansion?

No. Just one answer, please.

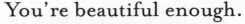

You're beautiful enough.

You're special enough.

You're sexy, playful, and fun enough.

You've worked enough.

You've cried enough.

You've been grateful, generous, and kind enough.

Okay, then? So what are you waiting for?

Give it to yourself!

Your faithful scorekeeper,

The Universe

You see, I'm not the one who needs convincing.
Nor am I the one who's holding it back.

I didn't give you the power,

the glory, and the Kingdom so that you could just "eke" by,
be selfless, and make sacrifices.

I didn't give you dominion over all things so that just a few of
your dreams might come true.

I gave you these things so that you could have, do,
and be whatever you want.

Comprende?

A word on miracles...

Don't let those that have not yet transpired, blind you
to those that have. It really fouls things up.

Besides, you're doing so well for yourself.

If it weren't for your challenges,

how would you ever know that there are things
you still misunderstand?

You wouldn't.

Bless them. Embrace them. Give thanks.

Oh, sure. I could just tell you.
Ha, ha, ha, ha, ha, ha, ha, haaa . . . Ehee . . .
OOHHAAHAAA . . . HE-HE-HE-HE-HE! WHO-HA!
That was a good one!

Ahha! Found you, didn't I?

Dreaming you're human again.

Can't blame you. What a blast! You really know how to craft an adventure! I bet they'll even name a few bridges, or towns, or ponies after you in a couple hundred years!

Well, sorry to interrupt. As you were. Stay in touch, and be careful not to let all those adventures go to your head. Remember, nine out of ten angels temporarily lose themselves "dreaming human," because they begin taking everything so dang seriously.

Hey, you're good-looking this time!

What is it that

you'd really, really like to see happen in your life, but have not visualized in a really, really long time?

Right!

Well, let's just say conditions are now favorable, and it's time to rock-and-roll.

When all else seems to fail...

you can always help someone else, and succeed.

Met up with the dearest little angel
over the weekend, but she was so, so sad.

She asked, in the sweetest of angel voices, how there could
be so much love in the world, yet so few feel it. How there
could be so much beauty, yet hardly anyone sees it. And how there
could be so many miracles, yet most go unrecognized.

Poor thing.

So I reminded her of something far more important. I reminded
her that whether or not one knows of the love, one is still bathed
in it. Whether or not one sees the beauty, one still adds to it.
And whether or not one recognizes the miracles,
one still performs them, every single day.

Then, we both just beamed.

And whether or not these things are now known, they will be, by all.

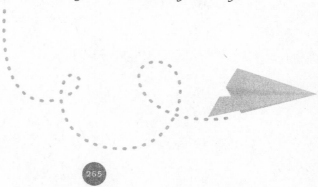

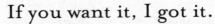

If you want it, I got it.

I got it! So why look elsewhere? To others?
To the things of time and space? Aren't we one?

Yes. Do your earthly things. Do all of them.
Move with your dreams. Not because of what you may or may not
achieve, but because you love life. Because you'll exponentially
increase your opportunities and because . . . you can.

After all, you are why "I got it."

Wherever you are drawn, go!
It's usually just me talking to you.

And the way you can be certain it's me is that both
your head and your heart will agree.

If it's not me, it's usually just laziness, or pride, or fear.

"God," how I love you.

*By the way, there's no such thing as the devil—and your heart
has always known this.*

Acts of kindness,
however small—a smile, a compliment, a helping hand—plant
seeds of hope, love, and beauty in a spectacular garden
you'll one day call home.

In the meantime, I'm enjoying the heck out of 'em.

Consider, if you will,

an enlightened soul.

Does Kwai Chang Caine of *Kung Fu* come to mind?
Certainly a likable chap, meditating and all that.

Now picture this: a being so alive that his vibrations heighten all
of his senses. His energy effortlessly summoning circumstances,
gathering friends, and blasting limits. Falling so in love with the
adventure of life that, like a child on a playground, he can't help
but stretch, reach, and rediscover all of his capabilities. Wanting
to be involved in every "game." Yearning to spring from bed each
morning to greet the day. Dipping his toes in every pool, stream,
and ocean, simply because he can. Understanding the power of
thought, and then sailing out into the world to avail himself of its
magic. Knocking on every door and turning over every stone to
facilitate the swift manifestation of his dreams.

Sure, you can do less and have more once you're enlightened. But when you realize that the world spins in your very hand, that your thoughts become the things and events of your life, and that there's truly nothing you can't do, be, or have, who would want to do less?

Have at it, Grasshopper,
The Universe

I know! How about a new TV series to improve enlightenment's image:
Gods Gone Wild?

I have a confession to make.

You know those folks in your life who you kind of wish weren't in your life? Well . . . they're plants. No, not the green, leafy kind. You know, stooges. Like "plants" in an audience. People placed there as if to test you.

I know, I know, I shouldn't have, but . . .
that's how much I love you.

The test is to not let them bug you. Can you do that? If you can, I'll either normalize them or pull 'em out like weeds, as you prefer. Otherwise they stay put, or worse, start multiplying like spring rye watered with Miracle-Gro.

Of course, I wouldn't have planted them in the first place if you hadn't insisted. And the test analogy? That was just an analogy.

If you tell them I said the weed thing, the deal's off.

You're simply the best.

You blow my mind. We're all in total awe. How you hold together
under pressure. How you face up to your challenges. And
your rebound ability totally rocks. You're driven, persistent,
and strong. Playful, silly, fun. Compassionate, sympathetic,
understanding. You're just plain unstoppable. And you always
have time for others. What a package.

Soooo . . . How 'bout cutting *yourself* some slack
every now and then?

Let's get back to basics . . .

You live in a dreamworld where all things are possible.

Your mere existence is the undeniable proof.

Hallelujah,
The Universe

Oh sure, you can knock

and it will be opened. Seek and it will be found.
Ask and it will be answered. But you could also just say "thanks."

And believing, you'll see that that which you stood in
need of was there all along.

What a system, huh? We call it built-in redundancy.

What a cool party, huh?!

Ever see so many happy, smiling faces dancing around like they don't have a care in the world? The food's from New Orleans. The chef from Paris. And the dancers are Bohemians! And how about all those helicopters and yachts bringing everyone to the island? What a trip!

Hey, it's kind of loud here, let's go down to the pool . . .
No, the other pool, by the tiki torches and palm trees so we don't have to compete with the bongo drums. That's better.

Now that I have your attention, and before we get swept away in the next conga line, I want to thank you. Thank you for being such an incredible example, and of course, thank you for inviting me to your party. You've really outdone yourself, again. Your home here is spectacular, your friends are a blast, and . . .

Oh my "God"! Isn't that Mick Jagger singing?!
You know Mick Jagger?!

By the way, what are we celebrating this time?

Get used to it.

I know what to do!
I know what to do! Send me there!

Imagine me as a whirling ball of gold. Going in and out, to and fro. Healing, helping, soothing. Understanding, showing, mending. Bridging, rekindling, befriending.

Let me be your doctor. Let me be your lawyer. Let me be your ambassador. Your *Niña*, *Pinta*, and *Santa María*. Exploring, discovering, and lighting the way.

Because there's nowhere we can't go, there's no one we can't reach, and there's nothing we can't do.

Hey, pretty cool to get those boats in there, huh? Huh? Huh?

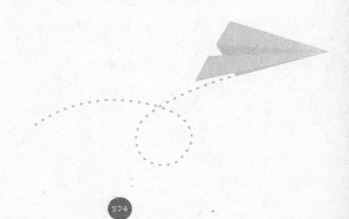

You know what's so strange

about walking that long, and oftentimes lonely, road of life?

When you reach its end, you won't remember it being
either long, or lonely.

Throughout your entire life

you've moved mountains, averted disasters, and orchestrated the
most thrilling of comebacks, clutches, and coincidences.

Hey, I should be asking *you* for help.

Do you know why,

even here, way out in the Universe, we love Fridays
every bit as much as you?

Because on Fridays, all of the angels regroup and share stories
of the remarkable heroism, incredible beauty, and heartfelt love
witnessed all over your astounding little planet.

*True, they do this every day, but on Fridays they blast that "Let's get ready to
rumble . . ." song for the weekend. "Whoomp! There it is . . ."*

If I had seams, they'd burst.
Limits, they'd shatter. Doubts, they'd vanish.
Tears, conquered. Worries, shredded.

Because I, your faithful servant and doting guardian, who hears
your innermost thoughts, who walks in your shoes, and who
lingers in your breath, can hardly contain the joy I feel over who
you've become.

Of course, you have little idea of what I'm talking about, but you
will. And trust me, you'll be overwhelmed, too. Had to get that
out, or I don't know what else would have burst.

Good thing I don't have stitches.

A Public Service Announcement

from the Universe:

Be on guard against those who help others in the name of sacrifice, selflessness, or altruism, instead of in the name of joy.

Because usually, they don't really help all that much.

Sad is the life that gives without realizing how much, in turn, it receives.

Don't doubt, hesitate, or waver.

There is no burden too great, no mountain too large, and no goal too high, if you do not doubt, hesitate, or waver, because the only things that can derail a dream are thoughts in contradiction.

Do you want to know

what's really beautiful? Confidence.

Do you want to know what's really powerful? Persistence.

Do you want to know what's really sexy?
(Please, I know about sexy.) Not needing to be needed.

And if still "they" don't notice your good looks, your strength,
and your sashay . . . could you feel more sorry for them?

Who needs Botox?

You aren't in time and space

to hit home runs. Couldn't even if you wanted to. Can't be done.
The logistics are impossible. And besides, the pressure from
trying would overwhelm the hardiest of souls.

Home runs are what I do. You just pitch.

You want a new job, pitch it to me. You want more friends, pitch
it to me. You want to lose weight, improve relationships, or strike
it rich, pitch it to me. There's nothing you can throw that I can't
hit clear out of the park.

Now, please, hand over the bat.

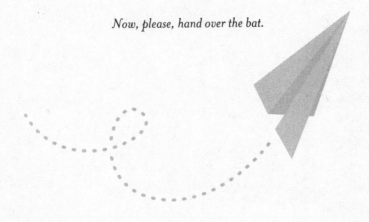

Enjoying short-term pleasures

at the expense of long-term dreams is just about as foolish a
strategy as pursuing long-term dreams at the expense of
short-term pleasures.

Pursue both.

If you take care of the inches,

I'll take care of the miles.

You just have to go first.

Okay, here's the skinny . . .

the answer to your question. The way, the light, the door.
The most overlooked truth in reality. And the one that requires
the most "uncommon sense" to fully grasp . . .

When it comes to effecting change (big or little, but especially
big), manifesting the life of your dreams, or getting that perfect
parking space, "thinking" is immeasurably more valuable
when used to imagine what you want—the end result—
than to figure out how you're going to get it.

Which is why most people have to schlep through big parking lots.

A coincidence?

Do you think it's just a coincidence that you look exactly
as you do?

Do you think your height, the color of your eyes, or the
sound of your voice were accidents?

Do you think your insights into life, your gifts of perception,
or your sense of humor were the result of random genetics?

Or, just maybe, do you think you're exactly as you now are,
with every freckle, trait, and charm, because they all added up
to how you could make the biggest difference with your life in
time and space?

And you're doing it.

Okay. Let's say you're walking

through the woods. All alone, miles from home, just minding
your own business and lost in your own wondrous thoughts.
Then suddenly, from absolutely nowhere, a huge grizzly bear
literally "appears" on the path just a short distance in front of
you, rears up on its hind legs, towering ten feet tall, waving both
forepaws high in the air over its head, and roars. Immediately
you see his large white teeth, his claws slicing the air, feel the heat
from his breath in the cool morning air, and you feel your whole
body spasm with fear as if you'd just been electrocuted.

Nanoseconds seem like eternity. Your mind wants to shut down,
but suddenly you regain control of the moment. Your adrenaline
is pumping, your muscles are primed, and your heart is racing.
Your instincts confirm what you feel in your heart: This "thing"
is mad! It's scared! It wants to destroy you!

What do you do next?
Freeze-frame.

Okay. Now, let's say you're living your normal, everyday life.
For the most part, you're a happy camper. Then suddenly,
from absolutely nowhere, a huge bill appears. An important
relationship stands on the brink of ruin. Your career of umpteen
years is horribly threatened. Or you just plain can't seem to break
through to "more." More of everything;
abundance, health, or harmony.

You're perplexed. You're angry. You're terrified. How? Why you? What gives? Your mind races. You want to put out the fires, throw a fit, wring a neck, and rail against an unfair world and the idiots who take you for granted.

What do you do next?
Freeze-frame.

Do you see the similarities?

Do you see how engaging your "beasts," whether you fight or flee, only strengthens them and lures you deeper into their spell? That when facing a crisis or challenge, the thing to do is be still, go within, and turn your attention away from it? The exact opposite of what common sense would have you do.

Easy? No.
Lifesaving? Yes.
How? Practice.

Speaking of bears...

You know how you're supposed to freeze if you startle one,
or even drop into a fetal position?

This makes you less threatening, and so the bear, after breathing
down your neck and roaring like Tarzan, will leave you alone.

Well, what if, when you curl up, you remain terrified? (You will.)

What if you doubt the effectiveness of your strategy? (You will.)

What if you worry and wonder whether or not you're going
to be the bear's next meal? (You will!)

Won't matter much, will it? Your actions will speak much louder
than your fears, and the bear will quickly lose interest.

Do you see?

You needn't worry that you sometimes doubt, fear, or have limiting thoughts about living the life of your dreams, so long as you are also doing what you know to do.

Pretending is powerful. Very, very, very powerful. All reality is swayed, even manipulated, when you pretend.

So even if it feels silly (it might), even if you doubt its effectiveness (you might), even if you still worry about "bad" stuff (you will!), still, at least once a day, pretend that you're making progress, that you're provided for, and that all your dreams are coming true.

Bears and I have a lot in common. Easily fooled by those who pretend. Only instead of leaving you all alone, I'll commission the rest of the world to play along. It's the law.

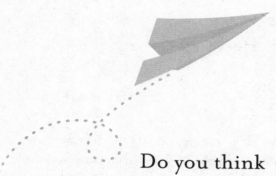

Do you think

it would be as much fun if you could trade some of the happiest days of your life for not having to experience some of the saddest?

Do you think it would be as much fun if you could guarantee that some of your dreams would come true, by forgoing others?

How about if only your "good" thoughts became things...

Or would you still want it all?

Ha, I knew it! You take after me.

xxoo

There are no challenges,

issues, or crises that do not contain within them seeds of
opportunity that could not have otherwise existed.

Bet you didn't know how lucky you were!

It's wise not to ask others,

not even me, for much of anything—guidance, help, time,
comfort, security, friendship, compassion, trust, respect, money,
love—that you yourself would not give.

Just a silly waste of time.

Give what you most want.

Adventurers Revelation

Here they are. The three pillars of reality. The Truths of Being.
The bedrock of your existence. The Holy Grail. They exist even
without a belief in them and in spite of beliefs that
contradict them.

First, there is only love.
Second, everything is of Me: One.
Third, thoughts become things.

Everything else, such as gravity, karma, relativity, and countless
others, are all subordinate and can be overridden or dispelled by
any one of these three Truths in the twinkling of an eye.

Can't imagine why I waited seven trillion years to share them.
Maybe it was because it took seven trillion years before
someone wondered. (You rock.)

Anyway, now you know. These are where I hide, like the wizard
pulling levers behind the curtain in Oz. And now you know how
utterly free, and powerful, and forever you will always be.

Notice that only one contains a variable?
That's where you fit in.

Protocol Clarification

In the adventure of life there are no "brownie points" earned for suffering, sacrifice, or tears. Nor for anguish, altruism, or selflessness. In fact, you don't even get any for generosity, gratitude, or compassion.

In time and space there are no "brownie points," period.

Might as well just do what makes you happy.

Their cookies are a whole 'nother thing.

No matter what happens

or doesn't happen. No matter where you go or don't go. And no matter who you see or don't see. Today, this week, this episode of your life, will be looked back upon with the deepest fondness because the time will come when you will see its glorious perfection.

Of course you can count on me,

but please, never forget, I'm counting on you.

No pressure

Long weekend?

Me, too. You know . . . war, chaos, and that new strain of flu.
Guess I'm watching too much TV.

You probably won't believe this, but I'm as powerless as you
when it comes to living other people's lives. A total zero.
I don't even know what's going to happen tomorrow.

On the other hand, you are as powerful as I am when it comes
to living your own. You decide what's meant to be. You can
have anything you want. And everything is possible—flu or no flu,
war or no war—shock and all.

Don't give away this power while waiting to see what happens to
the rest of the world, when you can decide
what will happen in yours.

The Universe

See you in the news.

Hey! You're in time and space.

You're kind of like they are, so maybe you know what,
I mean just exactly what is going on with people these days?!

Maybe it has something to do with global warming, or could
just be plain old plate tectonics messing with your "circuitry."
I don't know, but more and more often I'm hearing claims of
supernatural powers. I see folks dreaming like rock stars.
And come prayer time, the "please may I"s and the "if it's okay
with you"s are being replaced with *outrageously* high expectations.

It's like they want it *all*!

Well, whatever it is, it's about *dang* time!

Can you imagine someone

waiting for a rosebud—yearning to smell its heavenly fragrance
and eager to see its impossible beauty—yet becoming so focused
and impatient for its impending bloom that they become
blind to all the others that already have?

It happens.

Some of the things

you criticize about yourself are your greatest strengths.

You do make us laugh,
The Universe

In between taking notes on how much and why we love you.
Laugh, that is.

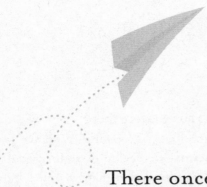

There once was a time

in your very own history, long, long ago, when the earth was a blooming paradise. The diversity of life on the planet was as mind-boggling as it was spectacular. Flowers sprang up in the wild. Animals were loved as family members. And complete strangers smiled and waved to one another, as it was everyone's natural instinct to be kind, to give, and to love.

Yep. Very, very little has changed since then.

See the good.

Of course, back then they didn't have the Discovery Channel,
so few knew how blessed they truly were.

You've done better

than you know. You've helped more than you realize.
And you're closer than you think.

Honestly, those poor Joneses.

Here's a clue

on how to know when new experiences, like you've never
experienced before, are about to transform your life,
even when nothing seems to be happening.

For the first time ever, you start saying and doing things
that you've never said or done before, even though nothing
seems to be happening.

Especially the "doing" part.

Now be honest

and think of all your dreams that have already come true.
A lot, right? Tons.

Actually, you're a bit of a legend here already.

Now, do you remember how before all the big ones came true,
when you were pushing, and reaching, and striving; hoping,
wishing, and praying, you'd think to yourself, "Then I'll be freer.
Then I'll be more confident. Then I'll know all things are possible!
How happy I will be!"

Hey, what happened?

It's working.

No, you probably can't see it yet, but I can.
Wheels are now turning that have never turned before.
Winds are now howling that have never howled before. And
players from every walk of life are being drawn into place as if in
some hypnotic dance. All because of you, your dreams,
and your divinely stubborn persistence.

If I wasn't the Universe, I don't think I'd believe it.

It's working.

Problems only exist
when one looks to the physical world for solutions.

As if!

As if you could change the story line of a movie by yanking on the silver screen.

All that you need,
to have all that you want, lies inside of you, right now.

Everything.

Okay, let's imagine

that the Universe is one big drive-thru McDonald's. And let's say
that one day, while tooling around, you find yourself very,
very hungry.

First, you drive up to the outdoor menu board, decide what you
want, and place your order. The point? You HAVE to make a
decision, and place your order.

Second, you drive your car to window one and pay.
The point? There's still stuff you must do, even after placing
your order.

Third, you drive to window two and receive your "Happy Meal."
The point? Your part is the easy part, but you must
keep on moving.

Point 4, you can always change your mind about what you
ordered, and though it may be inconvenient, sometimes
it's worth it.

Point 5, "Happy Meals" won't really make you happy.
But neither will anything else you order, though the act, or
journey, of willfully manifesting what you want totally rocks,
and will eventually remind you of your divinity.

Point 6, when you get what you want, everyone wins.

Point 7, the Universe exists to serve you.

I want you to think

of your life today, just as it is, just where you are.

Okay. Now I want you to think of the fabulous life
of your dreams.

All right. Now, do you realize that getting from here to there is
not something you can do without me?

I thought so. But then do you also realize that it's not
something *I* can do without *you*?

Awesome, we're almost there!

And do you further realize that the things I can do, you cannot?
And that the things you can do, I cannot?

That's big.

*In your every pursuit after your every dream, I am there. I want for you what you
want for yourself. And always, I know the absolute fastest way to bring it about.
But to use me, to engage the magic, you must first use yourself. Don't hesitate, be
bold, have faith. Imagine, visualize, and commence living the life of your dreams
today, to any degree that you can, and mountains will be the least that we'll move.*

Alakazaam, alakazoo . . .
That should pretty much do it.

You're now wiser than you've ever been, younger than you'll ever be, and less likely to wish without taking action, pray without having faith, and hope without remembering the magic.

Ha! Who needs the lottery?!

Helps to know the Universe, huh?

Now, please, remember your new skill sets.

You just never know

who in the crowd, standing beside you in line or passing you in
the street, might be raised in spirit, or even lifted from despair,
by the kindness in your glance or the comfort of your smile.

But they may never forget.

It takes so little.

The best shortcut

of all to the life of your dreams, is knowing that
you've already arrived.

Because you have.

There's always been something

about you that gave me goose bumps and, finally,
I think I'm able to put a finger on it.

Without you, who else would the angels point to
when speaking of "our kind—only braver?"

You inspire us each and every day.

With deep pride,
The Universe

No, I don't really have fingers.

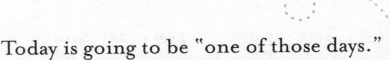

Today is going to be "one of those days."

You know, the kind of day that will literally unfold, moment by
moment, phone call by phone call, event after event, all based
upon the thoughts you choose to think, moment by moment,
phone call by phone call, event after event, starting right now.

You are so powerful that the entire world looks to you for
direction. (Well, at least today, because it is going to be
one of those days.)

Really, for you, today,
it's going to be like pulling rabbits from a hat.

If you only knew,

just how incredibly, wonderfully close you already are to
all that your heart desires . . . you'd be even closer.

If that's possible.

What would you call a reality

that turned the page of every new day based entirely upon
each individual's hopes and fears, thoughts and feelings,
words and deeds?

How about "easy?"

Challenges and issues and problems.
Lions and tigers and bears.

They're all just me! Showing up when you've somehow
forgotten—and need to be reminded of—how unbelievably
powerful you really are.

Because you will prevail. Oh my!

Of course, I could have just "drawn you pictures," sent you to workshops,
gotten you a tutor, but . . . oh, no. "I want to be like the others.
I want to make my own reality. You said I could do it myself!"
Ahhhhh, to be the Universe.

The "word" of the week
will be salamander.
Sa-la-man-der.

Salamanders were one of my ways of becoming even "more" than
who I was before there were any salamanders.

You know I could have picked armadillos, or tungsten, or
pink, because I was less before each of them, too, but I picked
salamanders. Maybe because as amphibians, they typically live in
two worlds. Yeah, they live in two worlds: in water and on land.

Are you beginning to get my drift?
Do you see where I'm going with this one?
You're kind of like a salamander . . .
(no, not because you live on land).

Thanks for making me "more" in spirit and in flesh.

IOU Big.

It's never too late.

There's no such thing

as too much gratitude. Because the more of it you express, the more reasons you'll be given to express it. And as the "game" progresses, you can rest assured that I will always "win."

You know that feeling?

That sense of eagerness for the moment. Optimism for the future. And confidence that you are exactly "when" and where you should be.

That feeling that makes dark days lighter and light days brighter. That precedes breakthroughs, conquests, and euphoria.

Yes, that feeling!

Well, it doesn't just come. You have to give it to yourself.

Go on.

If it helps, take it from me that you are exactly when and where you should be.

Excuse me,

but it's imperative that you read this one right away.
Lickity-split. Please . . . drop everything.

Have you ever thought to give thanks in advance for not "losing"
yourself when your ship comes in? Seriously. For remaining
grateful, considerate, and inspired long after the floodgates
open? People often change, you know, once the magical winds of
fortune fill their sails. And sometimes, it ain't pretty.

Well, not that anything is about to happen (I never tell
fortunes—prefer surprises), but let's just say, hypothetically
speaking, if incredible times were just around the corner for you
(or anyone for that matter, I'm just using you as an example).

New friends. Bellyaching laughter. Skipping, dancing, and
holding hands. A new fabulous home in the mountains
(shhhhhh, this is just a "what-if," don't get carried away).
I thought now might be a good time to tell you how much I like
you the way you are.

Close call.

One can never be too careful when the magic is about to be unleashed—
in general, you know. (So please, give thanks for not losing yourself in advance.
There's not much time left!)

If, way down deep,

you can even slightly comprehend that time is an illusion and that
space is just a stage, then it shouldn't take much of a leap to
realize how safe you are, how much magic there is, and,
most important, that there must exist a superconsciousness
with wishes and dreams all its own . . . that include you.

Let's get this party started.

It doesn't get any more beautiful,

any more magical, any richer,
or any easier than things are right now.

Until, of course, you start expecting it to.

At which point, I hope you have a really good broker.

Expectation summons legions.

Welcome home, dear chap!

Welcome home! Yes, yes, I know all about it. That's right, wipe
your feet at the door. Actually, there's a bath outside and you
could use a good long soak. Don't worry. Take your time. This
party never ends. Ah! Careful! You're dripping on this Note!

Oh, hi! Excuse me. Just welcoming back a fellow adventurer who,
well, who had a nasty little spill in some Amazonian quicksand.
Help was on the way, but you should have seen him flail!
Completely took him by surprise. And I do mean "took,"
which is quite all right. No coincidences, you know.

Hey, isn't taking the "quick" out of quicksand, or to paint
a prettier picture, simply floating in a cool sun-drenched
lagoon a lot like living the life of your dreams?!

The harder you physically work at it, the more you struggle to stay afloat, the quicker you sink. Takes some reverse logic to succeed. In moments of crisis—or bliss—instead of kicking and screaming and tossing out Hail Marys, remain calm and unflustered by appearances, stay focused upon what you want, and give unending thanks. Buoyancy, success, and the magic then come automatically.

Let me carry you higher. It's the only way to get there.

Okay, to clarify a bit:

You simply do not owe anyone, anything, ever.
Whoever they are, you are in their life because it served them.
It made their life better. This is what they wanted. You are not in
their life because they wanted to serve you. You can feel good
about this. It's the ultimate compliment.

Conversely, they are in your life because it served you. It made
your life better. This is what you wanted. They were not initially,
nor are they now primarily, in your life because you wanted to
serve them. You can feel just as good about this. It makes the
world go 'round. That's just the way it works.

And it's okay if and when your needs and theirs change.
This also makes the world go 'round.

Hope that didn't hurt.

You're free.

By the way, you've always made my life better.

So what if it takes a long time?
So what if it's already taken longer then you thought?
So what if it will still take longer?

The day will nevertheless arrive, as it always does, when all your prior efforts, determination, and persistence will seem a paltry price indeed as you are lifted irrevocably higher, as if by chariots of fire.

I can hear the music now.

I'm telling ya, I designed the system. And by design, you have no idea, yet, of the euphoric glory that draws ever near.

Would there be any point

in giving you the gift of imagination, the freedom to think
as you choose, and dreams that set your soul on fire if
even a single one of them couldn't come true?

I think not.

I love you too, too much.

Ever wonder

how many angels you have?

All of them.

They insisted.

You might never guess it

but sometimes, even here, we get frustrated. The classic case
happens at homecoming parties when we hear the guest of honor
lament, "Gosh, but I had no idea! I never would have guessed! I
didn't know I had such an effect on others! I didn't know I was so
responsible for my thoughts, words, and deeds!
I just didn't know..."

But it's even worse for them when we reply,
"Yes, but you could have."

*Of course, we follow that up with something much lighter, like,
"Hey, you look fab in wings!"*

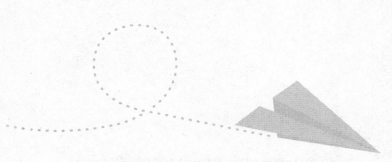

Would it make any difference

if you knew that we understand, deeply, the battles you've waged?

To know that we've approved of the choices you've made? That you have your own fan club here? That on the weekends we watch movie clips of your life? That every single morning we celebrate your birthday? That what you've learned, you've taught us all?

Would it make any difference if you knew that sometimes when no one's watching, we each, in our own way, pretend to be you?

Well, whether or not it makes a difference, you have.

Do you have any idea
of how powerful you REALLY are?

Do you have any idea of how far your thoughts reach?

Do you have any idea of how many lives you've already touched?

Do you have any idea of how much you've already accomplished?

Do you?

Whether it's praise,
love, criticism, money, time, space, power, punishment, sorrow,
laughter, care, pain, or pleasure . . .

the more you give, the more you will receive.

Has it occurred to you

that just as much as you now want your dreams to come true, once they have, you'll just as earnestly, passionately, and "badly" want to do, be, and have even more?

Of course it has.

So with this line of thinking, you also realize that you will never, ever have all you want, right? Oh, that's not so bad, it means as you constantly achieve, so will you simultaneously invent new dreams, just as you always have.

Brilliant.

So the trick, then, to being happy, is learning to experience it even though you don't yet have all you want, because you never will.

Nail this, and you'll be set for eternity.

Wasn't it clever of me

to think you up? I mean, come on, wow!

Never has there walked the face of the earth someone who thinks
with your degree of insight. Who loves with your degree of care.
Or who feels with your degree of hope. And never has there been
such a need for a soul with gifts like yours, because at this very
moment there are people only you can reach, and
differences only you can make.

Yeah, I must have been having a really good day.

Turn the jungles

of time and space . . . into a patio garden . . .
by realizing that their many mysteries actually conspire
on your behalf.

Today, you are a magnet . . .

for infinite abundance, divine intelligence, and unlimited love.

Actually, this has always been true.

It takes a BIG person
to accept full responsibility for their own happiness.

It takes an even bigger person to accept full responsibility
for their own *unhappiness*.

But it takes a spiritual giant who, upon realizing any degree of
unhappiness, decides to be the change they seek, in spite
of having to endure the "same old, same old" that may still linger
on for a while.

Yeah.

Fee-Fi-Fo-Fum.

By the sacred powers

vested in me—by me—I've decided to share the Secret Plan behind Creation (the SPC, shhhh!) with the most able, competent, and noble adventurers ever to live. This way, there'll be no more waiting around by anyone expecting to be shown their purpose and mission.

Ready?

There is none. How could there be, without limiting you?

Sorry. I can understand how that might tick some off. I mean, there's no one you're supposed to save. There's no hero or heroine destined to save you. And neither will the sky light up tomorrow with inscriptions as to what you should or shouldn't do.

That's the beauty of it. You decide these things, and you can choose whatever you like. But until you do, little else will happen, except that you may be buffeted about by the decisions of others.

Choose your horse, stake your claim,
and move with it.

To better understand

who you really are, understand why you want what you want,
getting to the emotions you seek.

To go even deeper . . . ask yourself why you think you can't
feel those now.

It's *not* hard.

Time and space are the playground of the Universe,
not the Harvard of the Universe.

Kindergarten dressed as paradise, at recess.

Ever wonder

how some of those who achieve incredible success, amass
fortunes, and enjoy sizzling relationships seem so unlikely?
You know, they're not that smart, good-looking, or even creative.

It's because intelligence, looks, even creativity, come in a distant
second place to believing. They achieved because they believed
they would, and so the heavens and earth were moved.

*Whatever I've done for another, well . . . just think of it as
practice for what I can do for you.*

While it's often thought

that happiness may spring from having some serious "bucks,"
it actually works best the other way around.

Your celestial financial planner,
The Universe

*It's not a trick of brilliance, or charm. Not wit or insight. Not health or prosperity
or popularity or depth. Happiness, alone, breeds happiness.
Just as it does all those other things.*

One of your greatest challenges
is realizing that the hurdles of time and space are simply
reflections of imagined hurdles.

See no problems.

All that you *must* do,
you've already done.

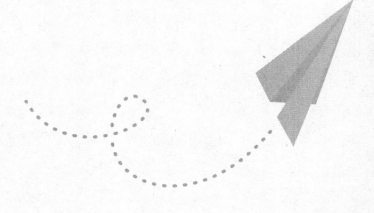

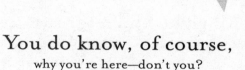

You do know, of course,

why you're here—don't you?

Because you couldn't resist the challenge.

Nothing in all creation, not in any sphere of the Universe,
compares to being born into time and space without any
recollection of your past; having to find your own way when lost,
your own courage when frightened, and the infinite powers at
your disposal when challenged; left to the elements to rediscover
your supremacy over them.

Driven by your passions so that you might rise above your
humble, naked beginnings, and ultimately see through the
illusions that had trapped you. To find yourself, once again, high
upon the throne of thy Kingdom come, whence it all began.

Either that, or you were dared.

All right, the reservation's

been made and a Beechcraft 400A private jet with experienced staff, advanced multimedia hookups for every passenger, and faux-leopard-skin sleeper recliners throughout, will be yours for any twenty-one days you choose. Just as soon as you arrange payment of US$368,750. In advance.

Fuel, of course, will be extra.

Now, repeat after me:

"You have to be joking!
Faux leopard skin is so 'early 2000.'
What else do they have?"

Cool. Now stay with this perspective, because this kind of transaction takes place every single day for those who already have.

And because perspectives summon circumstances
that change fortunes.

As surely as mountains

are to be climbed and oceans sailed, your dreams are meant to come true. This is why you're here, to live the life of your dreams. Not to be tested, challenged, and tried, but to conquer, champion, and rule.

Don't ever settle for less, don't ever think it's too late, and never, ever, ever compromise a dream.

Keep going, forge ahead, press on, and the day must dawn when your thirsts shall be quenched, and you, exalted.

If I didn't finally make that crystal clear, you'd throttle me once you got back.

Heartbreak,

disease, famine, and war casualties . . .

Can you imagine an angel who has only ever known time and space from a distance, who has spent the past few million years watching humans live their passionate little lives—helping them in and helping them out—ever wanting to taste the bounty of creation made flesh, herself?

Good. Now, can you imagine her insisting that her life be perfect, squeaky-clean, without challenges, without loss and the illusion of death? Or do you see her being keen for the full-blown deal—especially knowing that after each adventure she would be together again with all the other angels, in the palm of my hand?

Few choose to have their heart broken, to be infected with disease, afflicted by famine, or to die unexpectedly. And fewer still ever give these things *any thought* before experiencing them. But all have chosen and thought long and hard about the adventure of life. About being gripped by their passions and emotions so as to eventually learn of their divinity, to discover their power, and experience perfection.

Unexpected "misfortunes" serve merely as bridges to such ends, like steps on a ladder, not leading to the end, but to new beginnings in a panorama of BEING too unbelievably expansive for human eyes to ever see.

Isn't it grand?

Do you know what
you've been doing your entire life?

No, besides getting better.

Nope, besides getting wiser.

Noooo, besides getting older.

My, you are talkative today.

You've been touching, teaching, and healing friends and total
strangers every step of the way.

Lay on thy hands!
The Universe

And everywhere you went, the flowers gently swayed.

For those truly enlightened,

they have but to open their eyes upon making a "wish" to
see the entire Universe conspiring on their behalf.

For those not so enlightened, it's the exact same . . . except upon
opening their eyes they usually just see "stuff." And so they lose
faith, forget to give thanks, and are just too frightened to
"buy the shoes."

Pity.

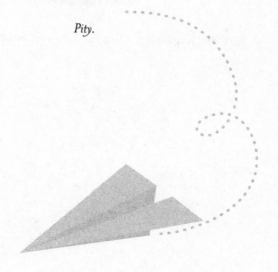

You *do* have time.

Someone bugging you?
Nah, way too easy.

Just like happiness, disappointment is an "inside" job.

Go for it,

not once, but again and again and again. Whatever it takes. Because in the end, with arms held high in the winner's circle, beaming with joy, as light as a feather, crying your eyes out, you'll see how fantastically disproportionate the rewards are for the effort expended, the risks taken, and the price paid—no matter how many false starts you endured. And you'll be astounded at how quickly you made it, even though, when the going got tough and your spirits ebbed, you thought you'd never, ever, ever "see the day."

Oh "God," I'm so proud of you.

There are a million reasons
why any dream might be considered irrational,
unreasonable, and a silly waste of time.

On the other hand, I can think of one that blows 'em
all out of the water . . .

We're in this together.

There's no breath you take, or step you make, that we don't share.

Do you realize

that the Universe cannot have, do, and be more...
unless you have, do, and be more?

Want it all.
(As if you didn't.)

To find the shortest path

to any dream, work with ideas, not facts.
Dwell upon the end result, not the hows.
And rely upon the Universe, not yourself.

There are some things

that are best forgotten. And when I remember what
a few of them are, I'll drop you a line.

But a couple of things worth remembering, that are all too
easily forgotten, are the times in your life when you felt
absolutely alone and uncertain.

Yet somehow, perhaps beyond perception, there was a great
click, after which, suddenly a new friend appeared, an idea
was imparted, or a connection established, causing the tides
to turn and the floodgates to open.

And remembering this, should such "alone and uncertain times"
ever revisit you, however dark they may seem, you'll at least be
comforted by recalling how transient they always are.

Pass it on,
The Universe

Did you just hear something?

Would a "forever being"

ever worry about the future? Ever look back and wonder?
Would a "forever being" ever have anything to fear?

Maybe. But only if they forgot they're forever.

When the hands of time are frozen and this world no longer
exists, you'll just be getting started. This is preschool.
Pre-pre-preschool. Let down your guard, go out on a limb, and
take some more chances. Experiment, play, and stretch yourself.
Honor your preferences, respect your wishes, and follow your
heart. Practice, try, and try again. Forget perfection, think
adventure, and do all these things knowing that nothing can ever
be taken away from a "forever being."

Sure, there may be a lot

of "real estate" between here and where you dream of being,
but the road, if you notice, happens to run straight
through the middle of paradise.

Behold, a new day . . .

with rainbows, sunshine, and blue skies.
New players, rebounds, and recoveries.
Abundance, health, and harmony . . .
just like you've been picturing them, right?

Right?!

Please tell me you've been picturing them!!

Goodness, gracious,

what are people thinking about?! Dominion over all things
doesn't come with age, spirituality, or even gratitude. In fact, it
doesn't come at all. You're born with it, and you now use it every
moment of every day, whenever you say,
"I will...I am...I have..."

And, for that matter, whenever you say,
"It's hard...I'm lost...I don't know..."

Careful where you point that thing!

You are exactly as you now are—

with your every mannerism, challenge, and trait; skill, talent, and strength—because before this life began, at the height of your glory, with full awareness of your divinity, reach, and magnificence, you knew best the choices that would maximize this adventure. Bad hair and all.

Trust yourself. You chose superbly, and though you may not see it yet, you've already mustered the courage you had to muster, faced the fears you had to face, braved the storms, fought the battles, and exceeded every expectation you ever had for being the kind of person you hoped you'd be.

Just tickles me pink,
The Universe

I think I'm going to put you in charge of the planet.

Always . . .

that which you most need is already at hand.

It's simply your incessant searching and belief in its absence that keeps it from view.

The only difference

between a friend and a foe is that you've decided where love can grow.

There isn't a soul on the planet who doesn't crave your approval.

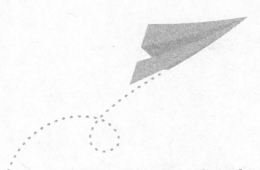

To make hard tasks easy...

mountains molehills, and challenges simple,
you can opt for one of two paths.

You can be still, go within, wait for divine guidance, and expect
spontaneous enlightenment.

Or you can just roll up your sleeves and get busy doing what you
can, with what you've got, from where you are.

May I suggest the latter? It's usually much faster. And it
makes you a bloomin' lightning rod for divine guidance and
spontaneous enlightenment.

Sometimes the most spiritual thing you can do is to get physical.

Imagine taking a picture

with any old camera. You pretty much just focus and click, right?

Now, does it matter how many friends are seen in the viewfinder to find them all in the print? Is it twice as hard to take a photo of two, or two hundred, as it is of one? Does the camera work harder to capture opulence instead of poverty?

Well, does it matter who takes the photo? Whether they're spiritual or not? What kind of a past they have? What their life lessons are?

Get the picture?

I'm kind of like a camera. I just copy what you focus on. And neither the complexity of the subject nor the amount of widgets it includes, nor where you've been in your life heretofore, makes any difference.

Cheese,
The Universe

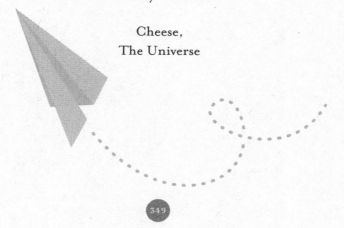

Report Card Day!

Here's your Report Card from the "School of Life."

Compassionate—A+
(gives of self, even when no one's looking)

Intuitive—A+
(naturally gifted)

Ability to see from others' perspectives—A+
(practically goes out-of-body)

Spiritually alert—A+
(aura beginning to glow)

Resilient and adaptable to unexpected change—A+
(like the Energizer Bunny)

Terminally optimistic—A+
(fast rebounder)

Exercises gratitude muscle—A+
(your cup to be refilled x 7)

Good-looking—A+
(a real hottie)

Patient and kind to self...hmmm—A
(could play a little more)

Visualizes every day . . .

Performs random "acts of faith" in line with dreams . . .

You're amazing! You aced the very toughest courses in time and space! Now, since the last two subjects are the easiest, you get to grade yourself.

Do you know why butterflies flit?

Fireflies light? Comets fall, trees grow, cats purr, and tails wag?

Well, I have some hunches, and here's my favorite: each is an aspect of the one who perceives them, emissaries of self, disguised by the elements, caught in an act of reflection, noticed in just the right time and at just the right place, to remind the dreamer, as if by metaphor, of their own sublime miracle.

Kind of like you are, to me.

Okay, so it's more than a hunch.

Was just peering down
through your blue skies this morning. Unbelievable!

Do you see the same when you look up? Crystal clear, azure, indigo, cobalt-kind-of-magical? There really are no words for it. *Lovely* even pales. And to think you get to live under it every single day of your life, knowing that even with the cloudiest and dreariest weather, just above the mist there exists such iridescent splendor. As if to hint at what forever might look like, to remind you of your infinite reach, and to make clear life's perfection.

Because if such beauty can exist in the sky alone, with only a palette of blue, imagine what else this artist can do.

Sometimes, to be honest, it's all so beautiful it makes my heart skip.

Oh, dearie me, of course I have a heart!
And when it's not skipping or jumping for joy, it's beating inside of yours.

There is no greater weapon . . .
than kindness.

A smile, a compliment, encouragement, and compassion belong
in the arsenal of every Time~Space Adventurer.

Today, may you crush, kill, and destroy the fears you
encounter, in others and in yourself.

En garde.

When you get there,
wherever "there" is for you, probably nothing else will matter
more than wanting to help others achieve as you have.

Who will you first reach out to? What will you do or say?
How will you conduct yourself in public? How will
you show them what you see?

Better start practicing.

The Evolution of a Dream

Dream is implanted into brain.

Dreamer becomes thrilled.

Dreamer becomes terrified.

If no action is taken, terrifying thoughts grow into flesh-eating
monsters. Dream is considered unrealistic.

If action is taken, terrifying thoughts are revealed to be paper
tigers. Confidence soars, miracles unfold, and dreamer
begins to saunter.

Either way, nothing remains the same.

*Act! The difference it will make in your life is more than can be comprehended.
But, of course, this is also true of inaction.*

Brace yourself!

It's time for more "good news, bad news."

The good news is that life is just an illusion.
A playground of sorts for spiritual adventurers to learn of their
divinity. Where absolutely anything can happen, thoughts become
things, and dreams do come true. It's like the ultimate test pilot's
paradise, where they can crash and burn, and do it again. Soar
and learn. Rise and fall. Conquer and stall. Or just fly in circles,
sometimes on purpose, sometimes not. All while lifting the entire
Universe—every imaginable form of consciousness—higher into
the light for their tears-and-laughter-bought lessons.

The bad news?

You're the test pilot.

Our hero and ace,
The Universe

*Ha, "bad news." You're an unlimited being of light; loved and adored; without
beginning or end; invincible, unlimited, almighty . . . Bad news? I don't think so.*

Never trust appearances.

Isn't it strange,

how once you set your "gaze" upon something
or someone, you get to decide what you'll see:
good, bad, or ugly. Yet still, you think "it," or "they,"
has something to do with your feelings and moods?

Don't fight it.

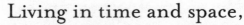

Living in time and space,

just might be the scariest, most heartbreaking,
and lonely path an angel could ever choose.

Until, of course, they realize that being scared doesn't mean they
can't make a difference, broken hearts can still love just fine,
and that feeling lonely doesn't mean they're actually alone.

Then they'll laugh an angel laugh, fluff their wings,
and dare a new dare all over again.

Love your halo,
The Universe

Anyone watching you?
Good. This is a double-secret exercise.

Pretend you just received a phone call with wonderful,
mind-blowing, life-changing news!

As you put down the receiver, your arms fly up over your head
with joy. Pumping fists, then waving palms, like you just crossed
a finish line before throngs of adoring fans. You cover your face
with your hands, trying to contain the euphoria, but it doesn't
work, so you reach for the sky again while shaking your head in
disbelief. You're grinning, crying, and just so happy!

Yes! Life is awesome, and you feel so grateful!!!!!!!

Got it?

Now, if someone catches you doing this, just tell 'em it was your
pet psychic who called, and they'll forget everything they just saw.

xxoo,
The Universe

PS—Show me what you want to feel, create the feeling within
yourself, and I'll then orchestrate the circumstances, however
outlandish, that will help you feel it again, and again, and again.

A question
from your friend the Universe:

Just how much time do you spend thinking big?

I mean really, *really* BIG?

Good, very good! Because that's exactly how
much of "it" you're going to get!

What a coincidence.

Your "challenges"
are simply the manifestation of your
so-called invisible, limiting beliefs.

Not so invisible after all, eh?

Life is like a dance

and we're partners.

Setbacks, delays, and detours? Heck, they're just like some of the steps in the mambo, tango, and cha-cha. If you dissected the movements and saw them without regard to the rest of the dance, everyone would look like total dorks. But when you see the big picture . . . poetry in motion.

In life, setbacks, delays, and detours are often just my way of "keeping" you for something way better. Don't let them discourage you, don't lose faith, and whatever you do, don't stop dancing.

Your most able choreographer,
The Universe

PS—You choose the dance, the ballroom,
or the disco, and let me write the steps, 'kay?

Bogged down,

spinnin' your wheels, out of time, frustrated, stressin'?

It's the details. You're messin' with the details,
which is a million times worse than messin' with Texas.

Messin' with the details is like trying to play tennis with a golf
club, like trying to cook with yesterday's hot stove, or trying to
find meaningful new friends at the mall wearing a chicken suit.

Just get clear on your vision—the end result. Think, think,
and let go. Follow your impulses, do what you can,
act as if, and know you've done your part.

The Universe is the detail Queen,
a perfectionist extraordinaire. Delegate.

Brock? (chickenspeak)

PS—Of course, there is a time and a place for
chicken suits, just not in Texas.

PPS—Remember what was just said about the details.

Do you want to know

what the world starts looking like when you start moving with
an understanding that you are a sublime Being of Light?

When you start realizing that you are the master of your destiny?
Knowing that all things are possible and that I do conspire
tirelessly on your behalf?

Yeah, pretty much the way it looks right now.

The things and events

of time and space . . . the stuff that's surrounding you now, your
memory of recent events, all simply reveal where you've been, not
where you're headed.

Oh . . . to see dreams abandoned

in the name of logic, for being unreasonable, impractical,
or pure fantasy, absolutely breaks my heart.

But just as sad is seeing logic abandoned in the name of dreams,
with the sometimes overly simplistic rationale that "anything is
possible," "thoughts become things," "dreams come true."

Ugh.

Logic has its place. Not because it helps depict the nature of
reality (it doesn't), but because it can help chart a course of least
resistance through a maze of sometimes hard-to-detect limiting
beliefs, thereby leading to an action plan, bolstering faith, belief,
and confidence, speeding up the whole manifestation process.

For example, let's say you dream of crossing a particular river
that has a swift-moving current, and in your mind you think it
can be done in one of two ways: you can either walk upon the
water (which you know is possible), or you can physically train
over a few months in order to swim it.

Now, how capable would you be of believing that you will ultimately achieve your dream (crossing the river) using either of the two ways? You'd be very capable. You'd believe, you'd immediately begin training, you'd find it easy to visualize yourself walking the shores on the other side, and it would be a done deal.

Okay, now how about if you were only allowed to walk upon the water (which is the predicament people create when they solely rely on the magic to carry them through life)? Would you believe in your dream of crossing the river? Would you be psyched? Or scared? Would you start moving toward your goal, or be paralyzed?

The funny thing is that in the first scenario, with your visualizing and believing (as evidenced by your preparations), "the Universe," depending upon your other beliefs, might intervene and whisk you across the river in ways you hadn't even known were possible, maybe even sending you a new best friend who could point out a nearby footbridge (I do that kind of thing, you know).

But for the poor chap who insists upon the magic carrying him across... Well, he's likely still sitting on the bank, chanting, and oommming, and visualizing. Burning incense, sporting henna tattoos, even telling passersby about the magic. But having a heck of a time truly believing that he can walk on water.

(One more page...)

The other funny thing is that having crossed the river via conventional methods, having mixed in a bit of logic with your approach, and having met with your inevitable success, now more than ever you understand that "anything is possible." That "thoughts become things." And that "dreams do come true." Far more so than the theoretical guru who still sits at the water's edge.

Sometimes it's spiritual to get logical. To do the obvious. To pound the pavement, knock on doors, spread the word. Besides, it sure beats just sitting around waiting to win the lottery. Expecting to meet your soul mate at the mall. Or planning to be discovered at Starbucks.

If you're already walking on water, please just forward this Note to someone who's not.

Ain't it grand?

You know, all the people, millions and millions and millions, who have gorgeous bodies that fill them with pride. Who've created enormous wealth—more than they could ever spend. Who have loving friends scattered all over the globe.

All because they just didn't take "no" for an answer.

Think about it,
The Universe

Can you keep a secret?

You know the space between you and all things, the void.

Like right now, the space between you and this book.

That's where I hide . . . and watch. Looking to see what your expectations are: of yourself, others, abundance, health, and happiness. And from this space . . . as I catch your thoughts, hear your words, and see all you do, no matter where we are . . .

I manifest the next moment in time.

Tallyho,
The Universe

PS—If you reach out now, into this space, you can feel me. I'm here. It's true. You're never alone.

Do you realize,

that you have never heard anything, from anyone,
that you did not want to hear?

Pretty tricky of you.

If there was just one thing

I could tell you about living the life of your dreams,
knowing that if you understood it, it would be "enough,"
I would ask you to realize that you already are.

Pssst . . . it's me again . . .
the Universe.

You deserve more, you know, much more.

And I just happen to have "some." Imagine.

Try this. STOP trying to predict, and therefore limit, where it's going to come from. Just know it's going to come and let me figure out the rest.

Cool?

By the way, you rock.
Shhhhh . . .

It's easy to look around

at all the people who already have what you want, notice how they
differ from you, and then think that they are the "kind of people"
for whom having what you want comes naturally. Whereas you are
not, otherwise you'd have it, too.

Very rational thinking, and a super way for non-adventurers to
avoid responsibility, rest on the sidelines, and watch more TV.

Adventurers, on the other hand, understand that they are
exactly the kind of people who should have the things they want.
Otherwise, they wouldn't be blessed with wanting them.

Would a loving parent

ever give a child a story to read that didn't have a
wonderfully happy ending?

No. Never. But they might add, "Whatever you do, don't stop
reading at the scary parts!"

Impatience is what you feel

when you think the future—in hours, days, or years—
will be "better" than the present.

It won't.

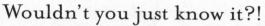

Wouldn't you just know it?!

You go to earth for a little adventure, some fun and games, some learning and growing, and the next thing you know, you're trapped in a sea of illusions, trying to figure everything out with a little human brain, sweating the details, and desperately seeking approval and appreciation.

Sounds like reality TV, except you can't vote anyone off.

Here's what you do: You remember how things really work.

You remember that the thoughts you choose to focus on, from this day forward, will become the things and events of the rest of your life, no matter where you've been, no matter what anyone else says, and no matter how scary things may seem to be.

You are "here" (your life now)

and you want to go "there" (your dreamed-of life). And because both are physical places, it would seem that you must manipulate the physical world to go from "here" to "there."

Aha! This is the ultimate illusion.

Physical places are simply mirages, reflections of an inner world, the world of your thoughts. So to get from "here" to "there" you must do your manipulating within.

A thought worth dwelling on—brought to you by your friend, the Universe.

If you only knew,

just how incredibly well everything is going to turn out, for you and those close to you, right now you'd likely feel light as a feather, free as the wind, happy, confident, giddy.

Whoops, kind of let the cat out of the bag there.

Well, now you know.

Know what's missing

from most people's lives?

The realization that nothing is missing from their lives.

The root of every "evil"

is looking to time and space for meaning, for solutions,
for identity; for friends, love, and laughter;
wealth, health, and harmony.

The source of all things—material things—is spirit, which is
molded by thought (yours) and then, without judgment,
impressed upon matter before your very eyes. Trying to get
what you want, no matter what it is, by looking to time and
space first is like putting the cart before the horse and will
leave you feeling powerless, heartbroken, even sick.

And dear heart, this is the candy-coated version of the truth.

Tallyho,
The Universe

Behold, a Being of Light,

radiant, illuminated, and full of grace. Come to lift humanity
higher into the light. All bow and sing praise . . .

Agh! It's you! What are you doing back in time and space?

Aha. I see. Pretending. Well, that's perfectly understandable.
We all need to pretend once in awhile.

So how's it going?

Yes, indeed, challenges. Part and parcel of any worthwhile
adventure. Tell me—there's a rumor that in time and space, the
illusions are soooooo captivating, the coffee soooooo rich, and
the chocolate soooooo dark, it's easy to forget you're just making
it all up and that all you have to do to awaken is to pretend your
way to wherever it is you'd like to go.

Cream and sugar?

Challenges in life

don't arise haphazardly, no matter how accidental or
coincidental they may seem. They only arrive when you're ready
for them. Not when you're ready to be squashed, but when you're
ready to grow, overcome, and be more than who you were
before they arrived.

The reason that some

of your thoughts haven't yet become things . . .

is because other thoughts of yours have.

Dearest Dear Heart,

I'm sorry to write you like this, but it's just not enough that
you tell me you adore me. That you love my mysterious ways and
that you're brimming with excitement for the infinite possibilities
that lay before us. It's simply not enough, not for me
and not for you. Pumpkin, you must show me.

You must go out into the world and greet each day with faith that
I am with you. Engage the magic.

Stride confidently into your affairs expecting a miracle,
and go boldly in the direction of your dreams.

Darling, it's time to ratchet things up a notch. Time to play, too,
to take everything less seriously, to get our "groove on," because
there's simply nothing, nothing, nothing that we cannot do
together... though it's you, Sunshine, who must
set us in motion.

Yours till the end of time,
The Universe

PS—You know, just do that thing you do, the one that drives me
wild. Be all of you... and the rest will happen naturally.
Uga-chug-a, uga-chug-a, uga-chug-a.

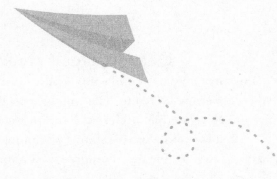

You simply have to change

your worldview—your opinions and beliefs—
in order to change your experience.

Tricky? Maybe.

Worth the effort? Depends.

How badly do you want greater peace of mind,
more friends and laughter, health, and comfort,
and enough abundance to never again have to ask,
"How much?"

Thinking...

is the ultimate contact sport.

Adventurer Alert

Remember... You are an intergalactic, indestructible,
unstoppable eternal Being of Light, and for the time being,
you're just pretending to be the little "hottie" holding this book.

Okay?

The Universe

You know, I think of myself

as pretty wonderful. So do many others. But I have to tell you that
I still field a lot of complaints about the nature of reality. Can
you believe it? I mean, life in time and space could not possibly
be any easier, any fairer, or any more fabulous than it is. But such
is the lot of the Universe, and that's okay by me.

Chief among these complaints are from those who haven't yet
won the lottery in spite of, they say, believing, visualizing, and
acting as if. Here is what I tell them, and I share this with you
because there are so many parallels, and perhaps one day—maybe,
not necessarily, but maybe—some of this can be shared by you
(when you start fielding these complaints yourself, of course).

Okay. I say to my people, "What you really want are bucks, dinars,
or rupees, right? In a word, abundance, yes? Not to win the
lottery." They say, "Yes, Universe." "And have I not often said,
by way of many, many others, that you must do what *you* can do,
all you can do, to help yourself, if you want me to do what
I can do, all I can do, to help you?

If you fish, go fishing. If you sell, go selling. If you teach, go
teaching. Because such demonstrations show us (me and you)
you're serious. They reflect a belief that you are not helpless, and
they help you enjoy what you already have—taking your mind
off of the lack. Right?"

"Yes, Universe."

"Now, if you want abundance, and you are as good-looking, and talented, and insightful, and resilient, and fearless, and powerful as you darn well know you are, yet all you're doing to experience it is buying lottery tickets, well ... have I made my point?"

"No, Universe."

"If all you're doing is buying lottery tickets, then not only are you not doing all you can do, but this tells 'us' there are other issues going on as well that aren't being addressed. And hoping to dodge them by winning the lottery is just poor planning. Because when I finally do pick your numbers and abundance showers down upon you like there's no tomorrow and your every cup, bucket, and tub is overflowing with bullion, jewels, and Hummers ... very, very little will actually change in your life, and you'll discover that abundance was not really what you most wanted."

That's what I tell them.

Your Sugar-Buddy in Adventure,
The Universe

PS—"There are so many parallels."

It's not real! Don't go there!

The things and events of time and space are like Play-Doh;
fictional, make-believe. What matters is what you feel in your
heart and the dreams that flit through your head. This is the
ultimate test, to discover what's real in a sea of illusions.

You can do it or you wouldn't be here. Don't look to the world
for clues, not even to your family, friends, or career. Look
within. You decide what's right. You decide what's possible. You
write the script and lay down the laws. You are the door, the path,
and the light.

Your invisible limiting beliefs

are only invisible when you live within their limits—or when
you keep on doing what you've always been doing.

Push yourself. Dare yourself to think bigger, to reach, and to
behave as if a dream or two of yours has *already* manifested.
Then you'll see 'dem little buggers pop out of the woodwork,
painted fluorescent orange, loaded to the teeth with logic,
imploring you to turn around and go back to safety!

Do something, do it today, something you wouldn't normally do.
Like maybe . . . take off early from work and go to a
matinee movie.

Aha! Did you just see a couple of 'em?!

Be warned: Sometimes, once exposed, they'll try to snuggle up to you, looking sooo
innocent and adorable. And as if that wasn't bad enough, they'll start with their
"baby talk." Sickening.

The best way to deal

with other people . . . is to just let them be other people.

After all, that's how you want them to deal with you.

Shhhhh . . .

The secret to living the life of your dreams is to start living the
life of your dreams, at once, to any degree that you possibly can.

Invariably, when big dreams come true,

and I mean BIG, there is a total metamorphosis of one's life.
Thoughts change. Words change. Decisions are made differently.
Gratitude is tossed about like rice at a wedding. Priorities are
rearranged, and optimism soars. Yeah, those folks are
almost annoying.

You could have guessed all that, huh?

Would you have guessed that these changes, invariably,
come about before, not after, the dream's manifestation?

Invariably means always.

Ahhhhh, let's see here,

whose day shall I make? Whose week? Year? Entire life?
Whose thoughts shall I endow with the power to become all
things? Who will be made invincible to every challenge, and who
shall I catapult over every obstacle? Who will get a second chance,
a third chance? No, not enough. Whose "life reset button" shall
I hit whenever they want a "do-over?" Who will eat their cake,
and have it too????

Oh, there I go again. Fantasizing, pretending, wishing it was
really me who gets to decide such things—dang it. Wishing I could
bestow such blessings, instead of just being the "techie" behind
the scenes allowed to perform my miracles and magic only when
called upon and believed in. It's like I'm life's Maytag repairman.

Use me. Please. So that I may fill your every cup, grant your every
wish, and harvest your every dream. And let's begin today.

Guess I had to let that out.

Love you, whatever you choose,
The Universe

PS—It couldn't possibly be any easier than it is.

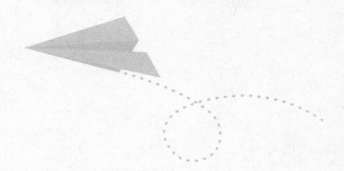

As powerful as you are . . .
whose day are you going to make today?

All things considered . . .
you've never really asked for much.

Hey, what's up with that?

When you look into the mirror

each morning, do you apply your makeup or shaving cream
to your reflection in the glass?

Ha! Of course not; you'd be locked up. Instead, you go to the
source of the reflection.

So then, when it comes to living the life of your dreams, the same
philosophy should apply. Why try to manipulate the illusions of
time and space when you can go to their source, the inner world
of your own thoughts, beliefs, and expectations, where the real
work is done anyway?

The perfection

of your every "issue" is beyond your comprehension.

Don't be fooled. You've made no mistakes. The territory behind
you and the challenges at hand were precisely crafted to
deliver the wisdom and insights that will make possible
the life of your dreams.

Get through what you must get through today, understand what
troubles you, do what you can, and all the rest will be made easy.
You didn't come here to face hurdle after hurdle after hurdle.
It doesn't work like that. It's not as if by mastering your issues
today, more will be added tomorrow. (That only happens when
you deny them today.)

Master your issues today, and be free.

*So little can yield so much. A new perspective, an admission, a surrender to truth—
however painful—changes everything.*

Everything matters.

It's not so much

about having faith in yourself. Way too hard.
Besides, you can wrestle that croc after you move mountains.

For now, just have faith in me, in the magic,
and in the unseen, and it shall be done.

Tallyho,
The Universe

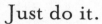

Just do it.
Everything you need to know, you know, and
everything you need to have, you have. Everything!

Time and Space is a primitive school. There are bigger challenges
"out there," bigger adventures, and lots more friends, but you
gotta do what you gotta do, here and now. You gotta live the
truths you've discovered, apply the principles, and never again
think, "Why isn't it working?" "It's hard," "I don't know,"
because such thoughts are like hitting the replay button for
whatever you've just been through.

Look ahead with your dreams in mind and give thanks,
because you know exactly what to do.

Phew . . . feel better?

Tallyho, ho, ho!

What if you did have the power,

the reach, and the glory? What if you were given dominion
over all things? And what if eternity lay before you,
brimming with love, friends, and laughter?

Yet still, one day, in all your radiance, bubbling over
with giddy excitement, you tripped, fell, and got hurt.
Really badly hurt.

Would you hate yourself? Would you give up on
your dreams? Would you forget about your power,
your reach, and the glory?

Oh, come now...

Never underestimate the Universe.

Here's a little trick
on how to change the scenery in your life
radically, fantastically, and, perhaps, forever.
(If that's what you really want.)

Look the other way.

It took some craftiness

to create the splendors you now live in, because it all had to be
done with the most exquisite balance, and in just such a way that
you'd never, ever become bored.

Yeah, I had to throw in a few valleys so that you could truly
appreciate the peaks. A few scaly, ugly, biting creatures, to make
the others more adorable. Some slippery slopes, dangerous
curves, and moving targets, to show you how agile, brilliant,
and cunning you are. And some quicksand, tornadoes, and
earthquakes, to help you appreciate a stolen nap, an evening
stroll, and quiet times.

But perhaps, best of all, I had to dream up some pretty special
people. You know, with perspectives and traits so unlike your own
that sometimes it would seem your only means of surviving the
relationship would be learning to love yourself, even more.
Aren't they a piece of work?

Oh, the sublime irony.

It all goes by so fast, doesn't it?
One minute you're here, and the next you're gone.

So really, you've got nothing to lose, have you? Nothing! You're gonna make it "home" anyway. You're gonna be exalted, and it's gonna be so glorious, happy, and easy.

Then, after a careful life review, you're gonna slap your hand on your celestial forehead, jump up and down with uproarious laughter, and say, "Dang, my thoughts *really did* become the things and events of my life. That little book was right. And as exalted as I am here, I was there. And as easy as it is here, so could it have been there! I wanna play again, I wanna go back. This time I promise not to forget. I promise I'll believe in my dreams and myself. I'll never let go. I'll never give up. I'll keep the faith. Really I will."

Hidden excerpt

from

Illumination for Dummies: Time~Space Edition.
Now a best seller in dimensions far, far away . . .

It's like, between every single second of the day, there's a pause.
Life is suspended. Frozen and unfrozen. Imperceptible to the
physical senses because these moments and non-moments are
all strung together by your thoughts, beliefs, and intents, which
span the gaps, creating a complete and seamless picture. It's even
happening now, between every word you've just read.

It's during these pauses that the future is forged. And just as
all things flicker like a firefly, so does time, during which I'm
busy at work, flying into action, moving mountains, plotting
circumstances, and planning coincidences, unrestrained by the
limits of material existence, including cause and effect.
This is where the magic lies.

Each succeeding physical moment then reflects the creations of
the previous non-physical moment, dependent not upon what
has existed in the physical, but upon the usually slow evolution
of your beliefs, intents, and expectations that carry through both
realities. (Are you sitting down?)

The past can even be rewritten and memories inserted, so that
never a beat is missed. (Scratch "can even be," and use "is often."
Just pacing you to ward off brain freeze.)

Next time you want something, play off these pauses, not time
and space. Don't look to the physical, look to the unseen.
And dwell in the realm of infinite possibilities.

But you knew that.

Tallyho, ho, ho,
The Universe

PS—It goes on to say that the evolution spoken of
need not be slow.

Oh, "it's" not working?

Well, do you know where you'd be right now,
what your life would be like, if it wasn't working?

Not reading this, for one. About half as good-looking
as you now are, two. And perhaps wondering, in a
strictly spiritual sense, who let the dogs out.

The Universe

PS—It is working. And it's getting easier.
And you *are* getting better, and better, and better.

If you knew for certain

that very, very soon all your dreams would be coming true,
what would you do today to prepare the way? (Do it.)

How might you celebrate? (Do this, too.)

Who would you tell? (Write them a brief note, now;
you don't have to mail it yet.)

What thoughts of gratitude would you have? (Express them.)

And finally, who would you help to "achieve,"
as you have achieved? (Help them.)

Adventurers Global Advisory

"Staying the course" should not be confused with
clinging to a cursed "how."

No matter how great the temptation . . .
(I'm talking about the temptation you're feeling right this very
second), no matter how great . . . STOP seeing yourself
as just human!

You are pure energy, with an infinite reach.

What will it take for you

to begin having full-time faith that there does indeed exist a
magical Universe that is, at this very moment,
conspiring on your behalf?

How about your ability to read my thoughts, right now, by
deciphering these little black squiggles on the page?
How about the fact that right now, billions of atoms and cells are
busy whirling about, while holding you together?
How about the fact that your heart has beat some twenty-two
times, without your help, since you began reading this page?
How about all the lucky coincidences and happy accidents that
have brought you friends who now love you and adventures
to thrill, with more of both on the horizon?
How about the fact that the sun rose this morning so that
you might have another day in paradise?

Hul-lo?

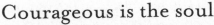

Courageous is the soul

who ventures into time and space to learn of their divinity.
For while they cannot lose, they can think they have, and the loss
will seem intolerable. And while they cannot fail, they can think
they have, and the pain will seem unbearable. And while they
cannot ever be less than they truly are—powerful, eternal,
and loved—they can think they are, and all hope will seem lost.

And therein lies their test. A test of perceptions: of what to
focus on, of what to believe in, in spite of appearances.

Courageous indeed . . . the pride of the Universe,
and I should know.

Whatever you'd like to know,

you already know.

Be still.

You are the reason the sun came up today.

Believe it.

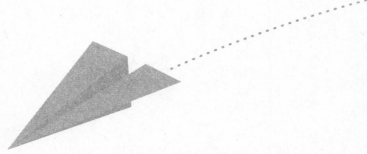

It's not possible!

You cannot significantly change your life, for better or for worse, by manipulating the material world. Not by working harder, not by studying longer, not by schmoozing, not by sweating, not by fasting, not by the hair of your chinny chin chin.

But change, great change, is inescapable when you first begin manipulating the world of your thoughts, which weigh a whole lot less than material things anyway.

It's that simple.

Wait a minute!

What does being a better you have to do with anything?

Nothing! You're already smarter, kinder, more honest,
insightful, and ambitious, even better looking, than 99.99
percent of the people who now live in abundance, health, and
harmony. True? You know it is!

It's not about being a better you, nor even a more deserving you.
It's about knowing you're already both.

Whosoever may torment you,

harass you, confound you, or upset you is a teacher.

Not because they're wise, but because you seek to become so.

Actually, it's pretty simple.

You have one real choice:

To do your best, with what you have, from where you are.

Everything else is just stalling.

What if, this very moment,

you realized you were dreaming? Dreaming you were at home,
at work, wherever you now are, and that you were reading this
Note. And in that dream you also realized that as real as it all
seemed, there was also a greater reality from which you were
dreaming and a greater essence that is yourself. That you came
from eternity and will return to eternity, and that, in truth, you
are your dream weaver.

Then suddenly it dawned on you that you could not
awaken from this dream until you first demonstrated this
revelation by claiming responsibility for your every manifestation
heretofore and exercising dominion over all things.

Yeeeeehaaaaaaaaaaaaaaaaaaa!

Have you ever wondered . . .

at how you might change, once some of your grandest
dreams are realized?

About how you'd behave differently if you already had a fabulous
house on the lake, or if you were suddenly surrounded by
mobs of loving and adoring friends?

You'd saunter. Yep, when you walked outside your home,
through the 'hood, grocery store, or office, you'd saunter.
You'd even saunter inside your home.

So start sauntering. Get into it. And maybe start winking, too.
Not only will people notice your calm, your grace, and
your confidence, but so will I.

Don't wait for those feelings

of excitement, confidence, and expectation that will come when
your life suddenly takes off, because your life cannot suddenly
take off until you first have those feelings of excitement,
confidence, and expectation.

(Heck, if you have to, just pretend. Make believe, fake it.
Right now, get up, walk down the hall, smile, wave, wink,
pump your fist, and exude all over the place!)

There's nothing you can ask for

that won't set the entire Universe in motion.

Nothing. Nothing. Nothing.

Just yesterday,

I was taking some time off, soaring through the sky,
spread-eagle style, flying between some mammoth cumulus
clouds, when—BAM—I flew into a stork on a delivery run.
Always loved storks, so simple, so accepting.

Felt bad for the poor fellow, so we flew together awhile and
I chatted him up. I didn't tell him I was the Universe.

You know what he told me?
He said there are no accidents.

"None?" I asked, feigning surprise.

"None."

"Well, then, it sure was a nice coincidence running
into you like this." And after sputtering a bit,
he said there were none of those either.

"None?"

"Nope."

I asked him how he knew so much about life, being a stork and all. And he said there was a little bit of the divine in all of us; that we all know the truth about reality, and that by focusing on any problem or question, the answer is drawn to you.

"Get out of here," I told him.

"No, really. Take today. I was wondering where all these babies came from, when—BAM—suddenly, from nowhere, I just knew."

What if there really was a Santa Claus,

an Easter Bunny, or a God who picked and chose among those whose prayers He answered, who got to decide who was ready for what and who judged those He would either save or damn?

I know, I know! Everyone could spend the rest of their lives hoping, wishing, and asking, instead of doing, being, and having.

Tallyho, ho, ho!

PS—Think we'll get any presents this year after that one?

Close? You are so close

it's actually painful for those who know.

Poor "things." With bated breath they're writhing in anticipation, rolling in the aisles, imploring you to stay the course. They can see what lies in the unseen, they know of the coincidences and accidents that are about to be unsprung, and they know if you could see them, too, you'd be unstoppable.

Whatever you do next, please, think of your fans.

Never compromise a dream.

Do what you must. The fears, beasts, and mountains before you are part of the plan; stepping-stones to a promised land; to a time and place that is so much closer than you even suspect. Don't let your eyes deceive, for even as you read these words, your ship swiftly approaches.

Can you imagine

actually being embarrassed by the enormity of wealth and abundance you've acquired? By the peace and harmony that pervade your life? By the ease and simplicity of everything you do? Almost feeling the need to apologize to those in your life who have yet to awaken and harness the principles that are free to all?

Start.

Have you been there?

To that place of quiet bliss, of knowing that you're doing enough, wishing for nothing except what already is, exactly as it is, seeing the blue in the sky like you've never seen it before, watching a butterfly as if it appeared just for you, feeling so light that you're sure you could float, understanding the trials and tribulations of days gone by and being glad for every single one of them, feeling so wrapped up in the present that you couldn't care less about tomorrow, knowing that you're provided for, that the manifestation of your dreams is inevitable, and that the Universe flat-out adores you, reveres you, and wants for nothing, except to see your smile and hear your laughter?

That's right, very good, dearest. You're there now.

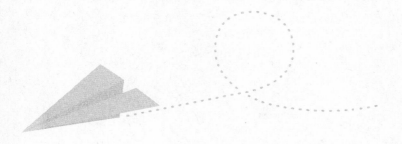

I need your help with this one.

Please, just for a second, hold out the palm of your hand and give it a quick glance. Now imagine a miniaturized version of a loved one carefully and comfortably resting in it. Feel waves of your love blanketing this precious being. Imagine seeing the life of this loved one playing out in your palm and feeling their every joy and sadness. Imagine reading his or her mind and wanting nothing for yourself except to see their dreams come true.

Then you smile radiantly, filled with pride and joy, knowing that they are always safe, always provided for, never alone, and inescapably destined to learn of these truths for themselves. You smile because you know that the day of their awakening swiftly approaches, as does their own sublime joy and the manifestation of their boldest dreams.

Okay, that should do it.

Now, can you also imagine that "someone else" right this very moment is smiling down at you as you play out your life in the palm of their hand?

Yours truly,
The Universe

Just like before . . .

it's gonna happen when you least expect it, from where you
least expect it, and how you least expect it.

So forget about it. Except, of course, to remember
that it's gonna happen.

Of all the people, in all the world,

not a single one of them . . . is more precious,
loved, and deserving than you.

Your attention, please...
Your attention, please...

This is the Universe.

Today I'll be recording your every thought and emotion, no matter how "good" or "bad," no matter how generous or stingy, and no matter how helpful or hurtful it may be. And everything I record... will be played back for you, as soon as possible, as some type of physical manifestation in time and space.

Thank you, that is all.

Adventurer Advisory Global Alert!

Do not trust facts!!!! While they appear to be logical and
self-proving, they are perhaps at the root of every evil
(if you believe in evil). Here are two safeguards that will help keep
you out of trouble:

First, do not ever look to facts for answers.
Second, never plan your life around them.

Facts masquerade as reality, when in fact (yuck, yuck) they're
little more than stubborn group opinions. Bad "facts"!

Just ignore 'em, and they'll go away.

You are creation's first and last chance . . .

to be you. Just as you are today. That's all you have to be.

Bask. It's more than enough.

It's always best

to assume that everyone either knows the truth or *will* know the truth, because either they do or they will.

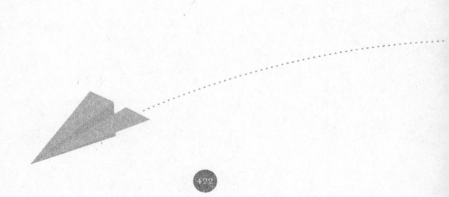

A little birdie

just came my way and mentioned a deep, soulful desire of yours.

Heavens no, not that one!

She said that you'd be eternally grateful if, once and for all,
you never, ever had to worry about money again.

Well, I couldn't resist. Wish granted! You never,
ever have to worry about money again.

Anything else? Anything at all?

The Universe

You could never spend

all the abundance that's yours to spend.
Your supply is truly limitless.

Of course, of course, you already know that. The size of your
supply isn't the issue. Finding it is. You know it's there, you know
it's yours, and you know you deserve it. But how to get your hands
on it? That's the challenge.

Aha. "How." Did you just ask "how"? You did.

Oh dear, never ask how. Never think about how;
let go of the hows. If you wonder about how, it means your
consciousness is not dwelling in spirit, it means you're trying
to manipulate matter, and it means you're gonna be
searching for a long, long, long, long time.

Steer clear of the hows, dear heart, and simply
dwell on the end result.

Got it?

For all the reasons
that you might draw someone into your life . . .
one would never be to find their faults.

Always, do what you can.
Because once you at least do what you can, no matter how
seemingly insignificant, everything changes.

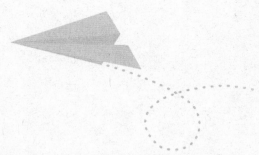

You want more, and that's good,

very good. More money, love, energy, laughter.

Okay, here's the deal . . . just remember that these "things"
lie only a thought away . . . not a career away, not a year away,
not a lucky break away, not a relationship away . . .
just a thought away.

Okay?

Now, please think those thoughts.

Do you have any idea
why I love you so much?

It's because if you were not exactly as you now are, for everything you've been through, I would not be exactly as I now am. And there are no words that can express just how much more I am because you are just as you now are. Oh ... Gives me the chills.

Wonder no more.

Your grateful comrade in adventure,
The Universe

Some Investment Advice
from the Universe

Did you follow your hunches during the '90s in the
stock market? Did you hear what I was telling you about huge
yields in real estate? Did you "stumble" across those itty-bitty
public companies with stock offerings that made
penny investors millionaires?

Phew, I was slammed doling out golden opportunities to anyone
I could reach. It became kind of a hobby, you know, to fill in the
gaps of boredom that go along with being the Universe.

Truthfully, though, you didn't miss a thing. Those fortunes
were chicken feed compared to what I offer on a full-time basis
through my day job. Are you ready for real opportunity? Do you
even have room for the returns? No, you don't. But that's
a good problem.

Thought. That's right. Thought is the greatest vehicle of all time for burying one's self, family, and friends in wealth and abundance—no matter what's going on with the economy.

Thoughts have their own economy, and now is a super-great time to get in on the ground floor. With my patented trade secrets, I can take any old invisible thought of yours and turn it into a mine of gold, a mountain of cash, a well of prosperity.

It's not too late! The best is yet to come. Invest in thought, follow your hunches, and live the life of your dreams.

Public disclosure:
This offer is irrevocable. You're now an investor whether you know it or not. All of your thoughts will become things. No lawyers can help you. Save yourself; choose the good ones.

Your wishes

are what the Universe wishes for you.
Your thoughts steer the ship of your dreams.
And no matter where you've "been," or how challenging your
circumstances, right here and now is all that matters.

You are forever. Invincible. A Being of Light on an adventure
of the highest order: to have fun and be happy in a magical,
infinite, loving reality that conspires tirelessly in your favor;
where thoughts become things, dreams come true,
and all things remain forever possible.

Any questions?

It's time you learned the truth.

Actually, you should have been told long, long ago.
You see, there was kind of a mix-up.

Things like this are never easy.
But, well, to be as direct as possible . . .
You're not human.

Of course, you probably just think I'm being cute,
but the truth is that you are not human.
Not even a little. Not one speck.

Now, before you go all ape, realize, there's a bright side to
everything, and in this case, it's blinding . . .
You no longer have to behave as one.

Tallyho,
The Universe

Don't just see the magic,
engage it! Challenge it! Dare it!

Dream big, with every expectation that your dreams will manifest. Demand that they come true! You're not beholden to life. Life is beholden to you. You are its reason for being. You came first.

Do you realize that everyone,
absolutely everyone on this planet—grumpy office workers, arguing children, fickle spouses, the narrow-minded, the extremists—all think they're doing their very best?

So how do you get through to someone who thinks they're doing their very best?

How would someone get through to you?

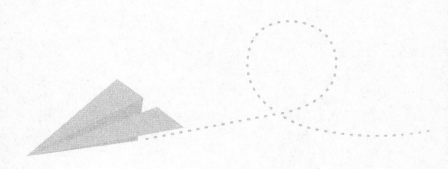

Amazing, simply amazing!

Do you realize that today you may or may not receive certain phone calls, compliments, emails, surprises, letters, or visitors?

Do you realize that today you may or may not receive word of good or bad news? Do you realize that today you may or may not encounter certain challenges, triumphs, problems, or victories?

And to think, you're the one who decides. Wow.

Be good to yourself.

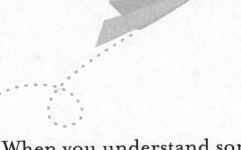

When you understand someone,

truly understand someone, no matter who they are,
you cannot help but love 'em, even though you might
not always love what they do.

You knew that.

Okay. Just as true is that for anyone you feel less than
love for, no matter who they are, it's because you do not
truly understand them.

No, you don't have to like what they do either, nor are you
"supposed" to stay with them. You get to decide those things.

Adventurers All-Points Bulletin

We interrupt your day to remind you that time is fleeting. Seconds, minutes, and hours are completely vanishing. Right now, here today, you are the spring chick of your tomorrows.

Cluck, baby.
Thank you.

Give.

Do not think

that you have to get "there," wherever "there" is for you, with
what you have today, whether in terms of money, confidence,
talent, connections, whatever. Doesn't work like that.
Too scary. Bad idea.

Once you set yourself in motion, the necessary resources—in
terms of money, confidence, talent, connections—will be
drawn to you.

[Soft whisper in the background, "Once you set
yourself in motion . . ."]

Fade out.

Did you realize

that whenever you gave anything, to anyone,
you gave to the entire world?

And did you realize that for every path you've walked, for
every stone you've turned over, and for every door you've
knocked on, you did so for everyone?

And finally, did you realize that whenever you felt love,
for any reason whatsoever, you irrevocably lifted the
entire planet higher into the light?

Thanks, from all of us.

If it's hard,

there's something you're missing.

For as long

as you are capable of anger, there are lessons to learn.

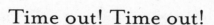

Time out! Time out!

What do you mean, it doesn't seem like it's working?
You can't see your life turning around?
It's hard? Ack!

Of course, it doesn't seem like that; of course, it seems hard!
This is an adventure, you're an adventurer, and uncertainty and
setbacks "happen." Besides, "easy" has never been your style,
and setbacks are only ever stepping-stones to grander places.

The day your ship arrives, and it now swiftly approaches, the
journey and the setbacks will be among your fondest memories.

Stay the course!

Resume play,
The Universe

PS—Challenges? Problems? Big deal!

Do you know what happens

just before something really incredible takes place? Something
mind-blowing? Just before a really huge dream comes true?

Do you?

Nothing.

Nothing happens. At least not in the physical world.

So if, perchance, right now, it appears that absolutely
nothing is happening in your life . . . consider it a sign.

The real reason you chose
to be here—your purpose and mission in life—
was to simply be who you now are.

Good reason.

The trick with imagination,
is remembering to use it.

Visualize every day.

This is the Universe,

and as part of this week's celebrations, I'm going to share a little
secret with you. Actually, I should have shared it with you ages
ago, but most "people" aren't ready for this kind of secret.
I've decided you're different.

It's the secret to getting anything, absolutely anything you want.
Okay? To magnetizing into your life the things, emotions, and
circumstances you dream of. All right? It explains how masters
become masters and adepts become adepts. And it'll finally
convince you that I am always there to lend a hand or perform
a miracle. Cool?

Practice.

Yeah, practice. Because just a little practice goes farther
than you could ever imagine.

Now fight the temptation to nod and shrug it off.
Do something! Visualize just a little. Act with faith just a little.
Explore your beliefs just a little. Manifest a little something;
a phone call, a compliment, a flower, whatever. Expect a little
miracle. Expect a little help. Expect it to be easy.

Practice.

What if there was only you,

and the rest of the world was "make-believe," imagination?
If even the people in your life were drawn there, or faded away,
based upon your thoughts.

Would it then be easier for you to grasp the true meaning of
limitless? Would you then believe that you alone
make your reality?

Dearest, the rest of the world is "make-believe," imagination.
And all the people in your life are there or fade away based upon
your thoughts.

WOW . . . that was easy.

Tallyho, limitless.

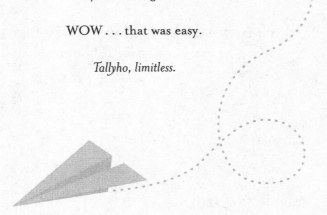

The reason you're "here"

is not to be good, to be better, to be perfect, to get "stuff" done,
to save the world, to save somebody, to prove something,
or to be anything . . . other than *yourself*.

That's all you have to work on. That's all you can do. But by
doing it . . . all those other things will happen anyway.

Your supply is the Universe,

and its ways are infinite.

You chose your dreams

for the journeys they'd inspire, and you knew when you chose
them that there'd be obstacles, dark days, and knuckleheads
who'd stand in your way. They're part and parcel of where
you're headed, and they don't just go away.

So when you face your next challenge, welcome it. Rise up,
don't back down. See it as a stepping-stone, not a wall; a valley,
not an abyss. And before you know it, as one is conquered after
another, the journey will be complete, and the joy of manifesting
your dream will pale in comparison to the satisfaction of your
persevering, overcoming, and breaking through.

Don't you see? These are the days, right now, mid-adventure,
that will mean the most to you once your dreams come true.

Enjoy.

Yo! This is the Universe,

and have I got great news!

I've just finished distributing the Powerball earnings and have lots and lots of time and energy and abundance left over. (You wouldn't even believe how much if I told you.)

Here's what I'm thinking:
How would you like more money, more time, and more friends? Yes?! Well, that's exactly what I've been working on!

Now, here's what you can do. At some point today, or during the week, take out a pen and paper (or use your computer if you like) and write a letter to someone who lives far away. Someone you love and respect, and share the "news" with them.

I want you to write this letter as if these dreams of yours
have *already* transpired, and I want you to tell them the whole
enchilada. Write down every detail. Share with them your
astonishment, the ramifications, and describe your happiness so
that they (and I) can feel your emotions. Then save that letter for
when you really need it.

Hokey? Absolutely! A powerful act of thought and faith
that will affect the course of your life.
Yes! Yes! Yes! Yes! Yes! Yes! Yes!

The longer the letter, and the greater the details,
the more powerful the effect.

Your humble servant,
The Universe

Let's pretend, just for today,

all day long, throughout our every thought and decision,
that life is easy, that everyone means well, and that time is
on our side. Okay?

And let's pretend that we are loved beyond belief, that magic
conspires on our behalf, and that nothing can ever hurt us
without our consent. All right?

And if we like this game, we'll play tomorrow as well, and the
next day, and the next, and pretty soon, it won't be a game at all,
because life, for us, will become those things. Just as it's become
what it is, today.

Thoughts become realities, too.

Today, you will be challenged.
Challenged by the grand illusion.
Tempted to look to time, space, and all things material for
understanding; to judge your place in the world;
and to make decisions about your life.

Fight it.
Go within.
Remember the magic.
Be vigilant.

449

Someone once said,
"No pain, no gain."
And so it became their reality.

Bummer, huh?

If they're in your life,
love them.

It's so tempting

to look at your present life situation, at whom you're with, at
where you work, at what you have and have not, and think to
yourself, "This was obviously meant to be, I'm here for a reason."
And to a degree, you'd be right. But you are where you are
because of the thoughts you used to (and may still) think, and so
you are where you are to learn that this is how life works—NOT
because it was meant to be.

Don't give away your power to vague or mysterious logic.
Tomorrow is a blank slate in terms of people, work, and play,
though because it, too, will be of your making, you will
again have that sense that it was meant to be, no matter
who or what you've drawn into your life.

Nothing is meant to be, except for your freedom
to choose and your power to create.

Choose big and be happy.

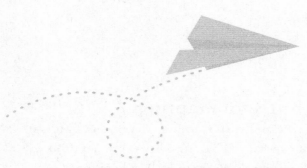

Do you think the Universe

ultimately rewards those who live in poverty? Do you think those
who toil and sweat from paycheck to paycheck are more likely
to inherit the Kingdom than those who work in ivory towers?
Does the Universe take special notice of sacrifices? Is it pleased
when some put the needs of others before their own? Does the
Universe favor those who strive to live spiritual lives?

Actually, honey, the Universe doesn't give a flying yahoo.
It loves you no matter what rules you make up.

Talk about unconditional.

Of all the joys on earth,

few compare to the crowning glory of achieving against the odds,
succeeding in the face of peril, or triumphing over adversity.
Wouldn't you say?

Yet in every such case, without exception, the poor odds,
the peril, and the adversity must come first.

Feeling blessed?

Be yourself.

Not who you're supposed to be, but who you want to be.
Not their way, but your way.
And everything else will take care of itself.

Dues?

Those were all taken care of eons ago!
You don't have any more dues to pay!

I know, I know, you don't believe it.

Okay, Plan B. You do have dues to pay. You must slave and
scrimp, wriggle and pimp, work overtime, pound the pavement,
sacrifice, barter, and be selfless. Endure the stupidity of others,
work a job you don't love, and unlearn a lifetime of bogus
teachings. Are these the dues you believe in? Well, then, haven't
you paid these, too, ten times over?

What good does it do

knowing approximately where the treasure lies, yet never digging? Having a bank account with millions in it, but never writing a check? Or discovering the fountain of youth, but never drinking a drop?

You must live the truths you discover, you must break your old rules, defy logic, be the change. Dig, write the check, and drink eternally, one little step after another.

I'm sorry, but there's no other way.

Tallyho,
The Universe

PS—Of course, you can ask for help.

Here's a little workshop
on how to manifest absolutely anything...

1. "Ask" once.
2. Give thanks often.

End of workshop.

What if it was true
that you make your own reality, and that your thoughts
became the things and events of your life?

What would you do differently in the next five minutes?
In the next five days?

Question:

What would it take, what would have to happen in your life these
days, for you to allow yourself to really kick back,
relax, and just enjoy?

Answer:

Whatever it is, *whatever*, you will achieve it, earn it,
acquire it, or experience it so much faster if you first kick back,
relax, and just enjoy.

Simple enough?

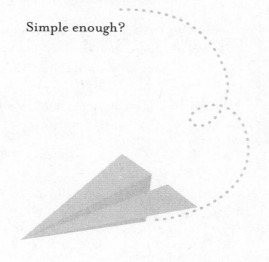

Good news!

By virtue of your brave presence in Time and Space,
an often challenging and sometimes even frightful arena,
you're prequalified for platinum Universal assistance.

This coverage is unlike any other on the market.
As a Time~Space Adventurer, you have at your disposal our
unlimited resources, invisible principles, and trillions of
years of experience, momentum, and overhead.

We can solve any problem, intervene in any crisis, and, quite
effortlessly, shock and delight the senses at a moment's notice.
And best of all, this coverage is free, eternal, and irrevocable. In
fact, even if you wanted to, you couldn't leave home without it.

In order to activate your coverage, simply give thanks.
Thanks in advance that the help you stand in need of
has already been provided.

Please, be our guest, enjoy these privileges that you
so richly deserve.

It does little good to say
you want something and then, "just in case,"
prepare to do without.

Burn your bridges.

Logic is overrated.
Big time.

There's always a way.

Let's play doctor:
I'll be the doctor.

"What's the matter, dear one?"

"Sometimes I don't feel good."

"Hmmm, let me take a look at you. Well, you look fine, sound fine, all your parts are working. Everything seems to be in order. Tell me, what kind of thoughts have you been thinking lately?"

"The usual. Trying not to let the turkeys get me down, keep my head above water, you know, stuff everyone thinks. Just wanting to get by, hold my own, survive."

"Aha, just as I thought. You've been thinking like everyone else,
so now you feel like everyone else, kind of *blah*."

"Well, here's a little trick. Stop trying to make so much sense
of things. Stop being so logical. Stop thinking that the future
depends upon what has been, or even what appears 'to be.' The
props of your life are just props, fictional. You're not at the
mercy of the past, the present, or the future . . . logic, reason,
or rationales.

You are a Being of Light for whom all things remain possible,
and there are no caveats to this truth."

Feel better?

Good.
Dr. Universe, Rx #77

You see, it's the same with everything.

It must happen in thought first. It must.
Even when, especially when, by all outer appearances,
your desires seem preposterous.

Anyone can think happy thoughts when they're happy,
wealthy thoughts when they're wealthy,
healthy thoughts when they're healthy.

Your life's mission was to create the stage you're now on so
that you'd have reason to awaken from your slumber. To have
dreams worth pursuing and the passion to press on in spite of
the conditions surrounding you. To learn you must look beyond
your illusions and grasp that your dreams are indeed
what's meant to be.

This is the Holy Grail. Your search is over.
Go out on a limb, give it your unending best, and never, ever,
ever give up. There haven't been any accidents, you haven't made
any mistakes, and the perfection is excruciating—you'll see.

Carry on, brave heart.

That's right. This is a dream.

You're still asleep. Any minute now, an elephant might appear behind you wearing a pink tutu and tennis shoes. Or maybe the phone will ring, and it'll be Abraham Lincoln to ask why you're late for the ball. Or perhaps Oprah is down the hall, live audience in tow, about to introduce you as her new favorite author. Anything can happen in a dream, anything, without regard to the past, without regard to logic, and you never have to figure out the "hows."

Learn from your dreams, because the stuff of time and space is no different. Forget your past. Pitch the logic. And drop the cursed hows.

Tallyho,
The Universe

PS—Cute whiskers.

The Universe knows how.

Adventurers All-Points Bulletin

Have you discovered yet how some angels—like the ones who heal
with their smiles, who help light the way for others, and in whose
path the flowers gently sway—are actually disguised as people?

And have you also noticed that some of them don't
even know they're angels?

Psssssst! This one was written for you.

Do you realize that for any

dream of yours to come true, the dreams of others take huge leaps forward? Not just indirectly, but directly. People like partners, family members, your agent, your reps, your suppliers, your custom-home builder, your publisher, and so many more. Even people you don't yet know. Then, as their dreams advance, the dreams of their associates are advanced, and then their associates, and then theirs, and so on, and so on.

What's really cool is that way deep down, they all know this ahead of time and they all know you. In fact, whenever you dream and move with those dreams, those among the masses whose own dreams are aligned with and complement yours are psychically summoned. Pacts are formed, deals are made, and coincidences calculated. Odds increase exponentially, and risks are minimized (if you believe in odds and risks). And you are propelled even farther and faster by their energy as well as your own.

In fact, I was actually asked to write this Note to you on behalf of all those whose lives will be dramatically enhanced by your dreams coming true. Your team, as it were.

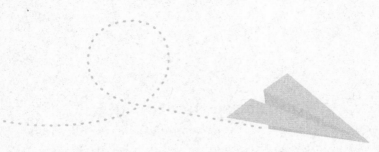

Can you imagine having

made a difference in so many lives that people everywhere talk
about you for the rest of their lives?

Can you imagine truly leaving the world a better place
than you found it?

Can you imagine that all the angels might know your name?

You have. It's done. They do.
Good God almighty, what are you gonna do next?

Just one of your many fans,
The Universe

PS—And you're so young!

All roads lead to truth,

though some will take you there a whole heck of a lot
quicker than others.

Be honest with yourself.

What if all the people

in your life, every single one of them, even the pesky ones,
asked to be there, so that your light might brighten their way?

Isn't it a hoot?

Of all the people in all the world who actually "get it," few,
if any, actually give it to themselves.

The trick? Baby steps.

Give, just a little, today. Give credit, give praise, give goodies
to yourself, and the Universe will give you even more.

Selfishness is a virtue, unless you think it must come at the expense of others.
And why would anyone think that? Oh yeah, that's what all the people who don't
"get it" told you.

Knock, knock. _____ _____?

It's me, the Universe, and I've heard a little rumor.

Seems someone on earth is asking for their own fabulous home
in the country!!!! Phew, wouldn't that be nice! Know anyone?
I thought so. Well, guess what? I have one, and it's ready
for delivery!

Would you do me a little favor? Would you tell them that in order
to get it from here to there, all they have to do is close their eyes,
count to three, click their heels, give thanks that it's already in
their life, and begin moving toward it?

No, no. Some of that's "make believe," but so is their
fabulous home in the country until they stop asking and
start giving thanks and moving toward it.

Tallyho,
The Universe

PS—Do something.

Don't let those

who aren't in tune with you, distract you from those who are.

How much longer

before you revel in the awareness that you are enough,
that you've done enough, and that you're now worthy
of your heart's greatest desires?

What has to happen for you to give this to yourself?

No biggie. Just wondering. Take your time.

Uh-oh...
Good news and bad news again.

First, the bad news. In the days, weeks, and months ahead you're very likely gonna have the same dang problem that you have today.

Now the good news. The only real problem you have today is thinking that you have problems.

You just don't.

The Universe

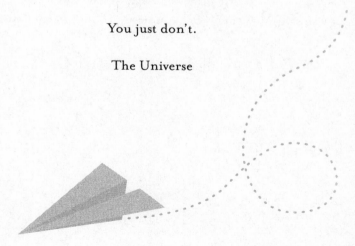

Here's a snippet of advice

that comes from an as yet undiscovered manuscript
buried deep in a Pyrenees mountain cave . . .

"Choose feelings over logic, adventure over perfection,
here over there, now over then, and always love, love, love."

It also said "you rock," but you never would have believed that.

Isn't it curious

how people pick others to be in their lives, at work, at home, and to play, not because they're perfect, but to have fun, learn, and grow? But then, shortly after they arrive, they're often unhappy because those they picked aren't perfect?

What am I missing?

No one in your shoes

could have done better than you've done, with where you began, what you had, and all you've been through. No one.

Aren't you glad it wasn't easier?

In life,

you can only ever be scared, when you believe in limits.

You can only ever feel lonely, when you stop doing things.

You can only ever become bored, when you no longer
follow your heart.

And you can only ever get overwhelmed, when you
think the illusions are real.

Whew! Who knew it could be so easy to get back on track?

The Universe

And on Friday, the Universe said,

"Yo! Ho! Ho! It's time to have fun!"

Whereupon it invented imagination, and there was a huge gasp among the angels. For it was clear that the reins of power in Time and Space had been passed to those so blessed, and that they would be left to discover this for themselves.

And it was good.

Happy anniversary!

PS—And as the angels quickly gathered, there, in line, stood you.

Can you imagine the joy,

the peace, the complete sense of satisfaction?
The harmony, the love, and stitches of laughter?
Can you imagine the interest income?!

Good, because nothing else shapes mountains, people,
and bank accounts quite like imagination.

Ka-ching.

It's the thirst for approval,

validation, and justification from sources outside of yourself that
blinds you to the fact that they need not be earned.

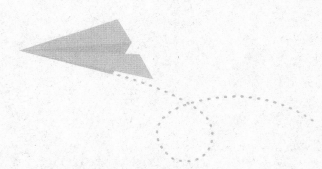

You wouldn't believe
the stuff people think they want.

Just the other day someone was asking for a llama.
Nothing wrong with llamas, I have a few myself, but the llama he
wants is supposed to help him with his business; schlepping stuff
over mountains. They're good for that.

Now, why do you suppose he didn't just ask for a pickup truck?
Trust me, he could've asked for a pickup truck, and he'd have
been a lot happier.

So . . . I'm off to the bazaar. In the meantime, should you need
anything, please be sure to ask for what you really want.

Imagine watching TV

and you see a German shepherd at the beach with a tennis ball in its mouth. Suddenly, with a subtle flick of its head, the dog throws the ball with pinpoint accuracy to its master 100 feet away. Or you watch a program where you see a Ferrari traveling at 160 mph, headed straight for a group of people standing in the middle of the road, eating shrimp and caviar, and at the precise point necessary, the car rapidly decelerates, abruptly stopping less than a single millimeter before disaster, and no one flinches.

What kind of TV do you watch, anyway?

Your brain wants to say "no way," because it wants logic and the physical senses to interpret reality, but the cinematographers have you in the palm of their hands, unbound by rules, free to play films in reverse, without telling you.

I am the same; my trump card lies in orchestrating an unseen reality that escapes both logic and the physical senses. It's as if I work backward, too. You think of the end result, what you want to happen in your life, and then I work backward, aligning your dreamed-of life with where you are today, stringing together people, places, and events, for the "impossible" to become possible.

This is how life works.

Trust me, I know how. Don't tie my hands with logic, fear, or limiting beliefs. And next year the "Oscar for trick photography" . . . could be yours.

Visualizing for Beginners...

For those who want convenient parking spaces, unexpected gifts,
or chance encounters with cool people:

First, think. Second, let go.

Visualizing for the Illuminated...

For those who want a healing touch, world peace,
or a new Bentley Azure:

First, think. Second, let go.

Choose carefully.

When you look at old photos

it's obvious, isn't it? You were good-looking back then.
Really good-looking. Yet somehow, at the time,
you didn't quite believe it.

Learn from yesterday, because today you're even better looking
than you were then. Way better. You're smarter, too. Funnier.
Wiser. More compassionate, less serious. And you're
finally sauntering!

Just thought you should know.

It's your degree of faith,

your belief in benevolent powers and events unseen, that
summons the magic, either in huge gobs or in drips and drops.

Go for gobs, it costs the same.

Just a reminder

in case you forgot, in case you've thought otherwise,
or in case you never knew...

There is nothing you can't have.
There is nothing you can't do.
There is nothing you can't be.

Okay?

Everything is optional,

and every option holds a promise, and in every promise
there's a plan for the "best of your life."

So, whatever you chose, or may yet choose, celebrate it.

To the conga line, "HEY!"
The Universe

Even not choosing is choosing, and this too deserves celebrating . . . "HEY!"

Did you know

that if you get happy enough,
you can actually hear colors and see music?
Paint without numbers? Eat desserts and lose weight?
Spend money and have more? Heal the sick?
Feed the poor? Love unconditionally?
And live forever?

If, you get happy enough.

I am,
The Universe

Okay, so you could already paint without numbers...

It's as if you won

the Universe's "Live the Absolute Life of Your Dreams" lottery,
a long, long, long time ago. But instead of finally checking your
ticket . . . you keep on buying more . . . hoping, wishing,
and praying.

Think of everyone

on the planet, everyone, as your special friend . . .
And so they shall become.

Dang.

Funny, huh,

how some folks think that avoiding challenges will
bring them peace?

As if the peace they now know didn't come from earlier
challenges that were faced and mastered.

Okay—not really that funny,
The Universe

The more challenges one faces today, the more "Whoohooo!s"
"Yeehaaa!s" and "Holy Batmans!" tomorrow.

Sometimes, lifetimes are chosen

to be with friends. And sometimes one friend agrees to be off
balance and the other balanced. One teaches stability, the other
teaches spontaneity. Win-win, cool-cool.

Gets kind of wonky though, if either starts thinking they're more
important to the other, than the other is to them.

You know?
The Universe

Every nut needs a cracker, and every cracker needs a nut, metaphorically.

Do you think

that the Universe longs to "Give you the Kingdom?"

Well, it doesn't.

You see, Your Highness, that transaction
took place absolutely ages ago.

Tallyho.

Here's the thing:

It—whatever "it" is for you, relationships, money, life—will never,
ever, be easy...until you first begin thinking of "it" as easy.

Chic-a-boom,
The Universe

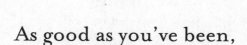

As good as you've been,

as on as you were, as high as you got,
and as easy as it was, things will still be better.

Payback, baby—
The Universe

Payback for your courage, imagination, and kindness to others. And even for your
propensity for kindness toward others, should the chance arise, which counts.

Remember,

you will always have friends, guides, and love,
but no one is coming to "save you."

That's not the adventure package you signed up for. You
wanted the one that comes with all the superpowers, guaranteed
rebounding abilities, and the all-powerful scrunched-nose-
when-you-smile.

Your 5 Star Time~Space Adventure Tour Agency Manager,
The Universe

Did you scrunch it? I know you just scrunched it.

What if . . . What if suddenly

in a flash of fire and light, you got it! And among other things, you suddenly understood, without a doubt, the creative power of your word.

Do you think you'd ever again utter, "it's hard," "it's not working," "something's wrong with me," or "I don't know?"

Nope, you wouldn't, not ever again.

Using your physical senses

to assess your options is kind of like driving while looking in the rearview mirror. Not too swift, unless you want to go backward.

Mostly, the physical senses show what has been, not what will be.

For direction, look within. To your feelings, your heart, and, most important, your dreams.

Though I must admit, you do look smashing in mirrors.

Whoa! Happy days! Rock on!

I just read about you in the *Universal Times*! THE *Universal Times*!
Sure enough, there you were, picture and all, ". . . this exemplary
Being of Light, residing on planet Earth"—I said to myself, "I
know that Being of Light!!"—"has been awarded the Double-
Secret Medal of Honor for bravery and valor in seeing through
the illusions of Time and Space!"

Now, this is no little thing! It's huge! Because even while
Time~Space is a primitive school, it's still the most hypnotic
adventure ever dreamed up.

In fact, only the most courageous are even allowed to participate.
And of these, only a teensy, tiny percentage ever come to realize
that it's all illusions; that they craft their own destinies; and that
in spite of all physical appearances to the contrary, any life can
turn around on a dime. Fewer still receive
the Double-Secret Award!

My word, you are extraordinary, and it's about time you
received the recognition you deserve.

But there's a reason it's double-secret. If you share this
news with lesser mortals . . . let's not go there.

Shhhhhh.

Tallyho,
The Universe

PS—You looked smashing in white, but what's with
the hat and feathers?

PPS—Now, remember why you won.

Your entire life is a work of art.

And as is true of all masterpieces, everything has meaning and is important, which includes your me-time, shopping, daydreaming, dessert selections, idle chats, and walkabouts.

One day people will study you,
The Universe

Let's just keep our ears on, okay? You do remind me of Van Gogh, sometimes.

Birds only know

their "is-ness," trees only know their "is-ness,"
and planets only know their "is-ness."

That's their only "business."

Let it be yours.

Knock, knock?
The Universe

Is-me, friend.

Do you know why you are you?
Because no one else could be.

Of course there are "things" you
want that you don't yet have!

They're why you're there.

Honor them, love them,

help them, heal them, but above all else, free them.

Everyone, of course—
The Universe

They'll return one day, somewhere, over the rainbow or in times without space.
And then they'll show you all the "pictures" they took, play some weird music, and
finally . . . they'll thank you. Crazy love.

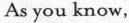

As you know,

for those already within time and space, their lives are so
often all about finding love and making money.

Yet not so long ago, while awaiting their first turn,
breathing would have been enough.

So much air, so little time—
The Universe

Hey, I vote for breathing, finding love, and making money, in that order.

Today treat everyone
exactly the way you would treat them
as if you had already "arrived," because behind their eyes,
the Universe is watching, looking for direction, as it paints each
moment of time.

Do DO Do Doo Do DO Do Doo...

Embrace criticism,
whether from the wise or from fools.

Never has a word been uttered that didn't have meaning
to those who heard it.

Do you know
what the former-living celebrate the most when they
consider their earlier times in space?

Not homes bought, cars driven, mountains climbed, or islands
hopped, but fears faced, hearts mended,
faith restored, and love bared.

A hearty crew (nyuk, nyuk, nyuk)—
The Universe

*Not that you can't also have a cool home on a nice island or
whatever other "things" you want, while you're at it.*

A Universal Rule
on Decision Making . . .

Don't make them until it's time to make them.
Unless you already know what you want, in which case,
however, there is no decision to be made.

You know,
The Universe

On the other hand, make your bed every morning.

Anger closes the mind

and cools the heart at a time when both are needed most.

And sometimes you wonder

whether or not you've been realistic, whether or not it's within you,
whether or not "it" really works. But in your wondering,
you've given pause to an entire Universe that never once
thought to doubt and yet still is poised to deliver.

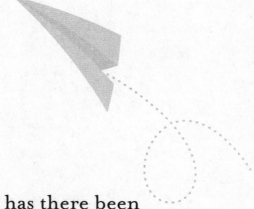

Never has there been

a moment in your life that wasn't also a moment in mine.
Never have you laughed without me, cried alone, or loved in vain.
And never have you dreamed a dream,
that destiny had not ordained.

Thanks,
The Universe

Now let's go do something radical about your waterfront home.

Some of the things

that hurt us here the most are your regrets over the past,
insecurities over downtime, and self-doubts over decisions to be
made. Heck, the past was only warm-up practice, downtime gives
us a chance to set a new stage, and it's you we call "the boss."

Born to run,
The Universe

Love yourself. We do.

Pop Quiz

Q: How do you find love, health, abundance, or enlightenment?

A: Stop searching. And start seeing what's been there all along.

There are no tough times,

hard knocks, or challenges that aren't laden with emeralds,
rubies, and diamonds for those who see them through.

Wild, huh,

how the entirety of living deliberately can be summed up
in just three words?

Thoughts become things.

Of course, beliefs are important, too, but your thoughts
can change what you believe.

And words are important—they're your thoughts that
will become things the soonest.

And taking action is absolutely critical, because it alone
connects the dots.

Spread the word,
The Universe

You were thinking chocolate, vanilla, and strawberry?

Fear, like joy,

usually means that you're exactly where you should be,
learning what you're ready to learn, about to become more than
who you were.

Whoohoo!!
The Universe

*Actually, you're always where you should be. Point being, just because you fear
something doesn't mean you should avoid it . . . usually.*

You—yes, you holding this book—
are the one who was sent to make a difference, to be a bridge,
to light the way, by living the truths that have been revealed to
you, so that others might do the same.

Now do you know why you've always seen the world
so much more clearly than others?

To help.

You are ready.

What if today was your day?

The most amazing day of your life, so far? A day that would
change everything for the better? What's already good would
become great. What's already great would become amazing.
And what's already amazing would become the stuff of legends.

And all you had to do to take advantage of the good and
wonderful things about to happen for you, was treat folks with a
true and eager kindness, think mostly of those things that please
you, and go out in the world, just a bit, where you could meet,
and mingle, and fall in love?

How much would you be clucking right now?

Beam, gush, preen! You got it . . .
The Universe

Today's your day.

One of life's most elusive lessons,
saved for only the wise and peculiar, is that there's
nothing, ever, to be unhappy about.

Unless, of course, you lose sight of the big picture, think the
illusions are real, or forget there's no such place as far away.

Whoot,
The Universe

Feeling peculiar?

The secret to getting rich
is knowing that you already are and acting like it.

PS—Darling, do tell me who manages your assets.
And those gems! Are they real?
(Answer: The Universe, and real what?)

All you have to do is be.
Be yourself.

There's nothing to prove. And there's no one to please who
isn't already over the moon with joy at how well you've done
and with who you've become.

This is the Universe,
and have I got some "goodish" news for you
(the "ish" isn't so good)!

The good news—you know the stuff you want: wealth and
abundance, friends and laughter, I think you once said a fabulous
house on the lake? Well, it's all done . . . hurray!

Your burning desires, the intense yearnings you've felt, the highly
pitched longing, and your silent pining for these things and more
have actually created this world . . . in another dimension.

(That's part of the "ish.")

In fact, I can see a "probable" you there now, lolling about in the
lap of luxury, giggling and then roaring with laughter, doing the
"lawn mower," high-fiving your friends, and them all turning
various shades of green with envy. You know, you're a real
hoot when you're so happy.

But there's more "ish." Seems the yearning and pining have actually distanced you from this reality you've created. You see, thoughts of "I want, I want, oh God, how I want" are picked up by the Universe, me, as "I don't have, I don't have, oh God, how I don't have," and then these thoughts manifest, as all thoughts do, perpetuating the lack!

To remove the "ish," here's the dish: Start with the "thank you, thank you, oh God, thank you," and behave accordingly.

Mow on, maestro,
The Universe

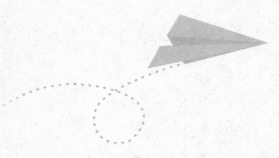

The Learning Game:

When there is ease and simplicity in your life,
it's because earlier you learned a lot.

When there is resistance and obstacles in your life,
it's because there's even more to learn.

And learning even more is pretty much the
main reason you're there.

Class dismissed,
The Universe

*You see, the "goal" is not ease and simplicity, though they
will surely follow, but learning even more.*

Usually, the best way
to find the yellow brick road of your life is to start out on
the dusty, dirt one.

And then let yourself become so preoccupied in making the best
of it, having fun, and challenging yourself that you actually stop
paying attention to the path.

Until, one day, not so long from now, with a new best friend,
wearing cool clothes, feeling awesome, a teeny tiny bit taller,
fresh from a WOW vacation, looking for the path you just left,
you'll notice that it's 24 carats . . . baby.

And you'll wonder for a long, long time, sipping on some exotic
fruit drink, when the transformation actually took place . . .

Tripping,
The Universe

Also wondering, as everyone always does,
"Whatever did I do to deserve so much, so fast . . . ?"

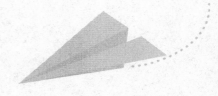

Someone so cool,

something so neat, and somewhere so wonderful are all on the menu. You just have to make up your mind and order.

And you should see dessert . . .

You must use what you've got.

Talent, brains, heart.

Instincts, hunches, feelings.

Money, health, friendships.

Time, space, stuff.

Otherwise, why would more be given?

You rock,
The Universe

Remember,

you're always granted lots of leeway, wiggle room,
and tolerance when engaging life's magic.

You just need to have a dream and show up,
then wands start waving all over the place.

Abara-shazaam!
The Universe

Aw-w-w . . . I love magic.

You could always

send a golden thought balloon to the most rocking possible
version of your future self, and thank them for reaching back
to you with inspiration, hunches, instincts, and impulses,
to help you bridge all gaps, connect all dots, and leap tall
buildings . . . you know, to bring about your quickest merger.

Love mergers,
The Universe

*And then remain open to the new ideas you start receiving,
no matter how crazy and outlandish they may seem.*

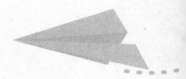

Limits are for those
who don't believe in the Universe.

It's okay to love material things;
matter is pure spirit, only more so.

Do you know why

it's so easy for us in the unseen to quickly pinpoint
your whereabouts?

You leave behind footprints of love.

Aw-w-w-w,
The Universe

The legend of BIGFOOT continues.

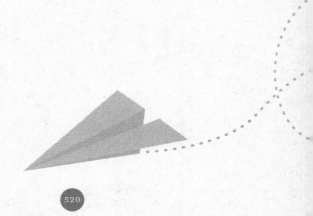

The secret to every success

lies not in what or even who you know, but in clearly
"seeing" where you want to go.

And going.

The power to have it all,
The Universe

*You were born with gifts of the gods and I don't just mean
making it rain. And yes, you can do that, too.*

Can you feel your heart beating?
It's beating in threes today.

Go on, right now, feel it.

It's saying, "I~^ love~^ you~^!"

And it really does.

Understanding...
is the elixir of life.

In times of great stress and great joy,
you are completely surrounded by loved ones
in the unseen who adore and support you, wanting to share
whatever you're experiencing.

So at those times, if you can remember to be calm and quiet and
go within, you'll feel them, you'll remember them, and you'll
benefit most from their presence.

"Look, she's smiling...Whoohoooo!!!"
The Universe

*Actually, they're there 24/7, lovingly carrying on, hooting and hollering, having
their pictures taken with you, each claiming credit for your piercing life insights,
your calm in the face of chaos, and your famed 1, 2 thingy when you bop to music
and think no one can see you...*

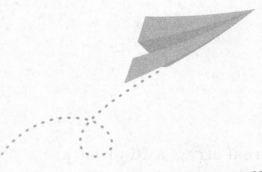

Dominion over all things

doesn't come with age, spirituality, or even gratitude.

You already wield it whenever you say,
"I will . . . I am . . . I have . . ."

Or, "It's hard . . . I'm lost . . . I don't know . . ."

I am you,
The Universe

Life's not about learning to find your power; it's about learning to use it.
And sometimes . . . chocolate, puppies, or purple.

If you could see

just how life was meant to be . . . you'd probably faint.

Because things would look exactly like they look today, and you'd find that you are exactly where you're "supposed" to be, in an adventure without end.

Of course,

"Here & Now" is what really matters, but people will be people, so . . . given that you're a Forever Being, I do hope you're spending as much time looking forward as you are looking back. Because really, forever means you have quite a lot to look forward to.

If the Universe suddenly appeared

before you in the form of a wise, old, kindly messiah with a
glowing white aura and presented you with a one-hundred-point
game plan that would guarantee, *guarantee* your dreams coming
true . . . but first required that you let go of all your worldly
possessions, shave your head, walk on a bed of nails, sacrifice
three hours every day training your mind, and invest a minimum
of two years before you began to see the first changes, would you
follow the plan?

Would you follow it if all of your dreams would then come true?

Did you say yes?

I know you said yes.

Now, if the Universe suddenly appeared before you on the pages of this book, spoke to your heart, and said that in order to begin living the life of your dreams within one year or less, all you had to do was imagine the life of your dreams (visualize five minutes a day), move with the life of your dreams (with a token act of faith performed just once a day), and honestly face your fears, would you even try?

Hmmmm.

If visualizing were extremely difficult,
maybe then people would do it.

Oh yeah, they'd form clubs, give designations, have car washes!

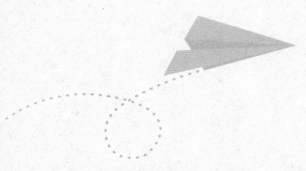

No more "supposed to"s.
Okay?

You're not supposed to work harder, look better, sleep less,
sell more, run faster, talk slower, be happier, stay longer,
leave earlier, cook, clean, negotiate, settle, start, stop,
move, try, win, shake, rattle or roll.

Other people made all that up.

I love you the way you are,
The Universe

Oh, you can do any or all of the above, you so can, but you're not "supposed to."

If summer resisted fall,

it wouldn't really be summer or fall.

Better to celebrate the season you're in . . .
especially those of your wonderful life.

Everything keeps getting better,
The Universe

Nice tulips.

Your attention, please . . .
Your attention, please . . .

This is the Universe.

Would whoever gave thanks for a home on the lake, more friends, and a couple of million bucks please specify which lake, what kind of friends, and provide some kind of general time frame?

Hul-lo?

Details. If they don't know, how can I?

You've been worthy.
You are worthy. You'll be worthy

It's not the career you choose,

the friend you marry, or the path you take that determines success or happiness in life, but that each day, in some small way, you seek to amaze as much as be amazed.

You "Wow" me,
The Universe

Oh, when we're this good, I just want to give you the biggest hug. . . .
Ummmmmmmmmmmmmmmh!

So-o-o-o-o-o-o . . .

How's it going down on earth? You know—in time and space,
where thoughts become things, all things are possible, and dreams
come true?! Are you totally kicking butt?

Oh, I see . . .

Yikes . . .

Uh-huh . . . .

Oh dear . . .

You don't say . . .

Psssst . . . I want to let you in on a little secret:

Everyone has issues. Everyone. Even those who don't appear to.
Because without issues, nothing would be worthwhile.

Think about that.

So glad we have these little talks . . .
The Universe

If time and space are illusions...
doesn't that mean you come "from" and now exist in a
"place" that "precedes" both?

Wouldn't this then mean that you're really everywhere, always?

It does, and you are...

Unlimited beyond your wildest imaginings.

The good thing
about bad things is that they make way for even better things.

In the adventure of life,

at first, no one gets it. So help is sent.

Then, over time, some start getting it, but no one lives it.
So more help is sent.

Soon, some start living it and even more start getting it,
and an upward spiral ensues.

Eventually, of course, everyone is getting it and living it . . .
But Earth's not there yet.

So the question to ask yourself is "Who shall I help next?"

You so get it,
The Universe

Act the part and circumstances will shift until it's no longer acting . . .

It's part of nature's

built-in checks and balances that while there may be times when you think you can't even help yourself, precisely in such moments there will always be someone else nearby . . . you can help, instead.

Which, I think you know, is actually one of the fastest ways to help *yourself*.

I hope that helps,
The Universe

I sure feel better.

When you stop and reflect

that thoughts become things, unconditionally, without exception,
no matter what, no matter whose, and you grasp that this is an
immutable law that throws the entire Universe into overdrive on
your behalf, don't you just want to cry for those who
still keep looking for answers?

Me, too.

If you only knew

just how literally true all of these Notes are—concerning your
power, your strength, and your divinity, about the love, the
magic, and the infinite possibilities—for the next few days you'd
see the rest of the world . . . through tears.

And you'd never stop giving thanks.

Ain't life grand?

And the day will come

when all of the gold in the world will not appeal to you
as much as having just one more day of being who and where you
already are, with what you already have.

If it hasn't already.

Thank you,
The Universe

*Not because your days will be limited, but because you've already
made such an awesome difference.*

To me, Earth is like a birthday cake
that excites me every single day.

The crust is like the frosting, and you are like a really, really bright candle.

Thank you for your light, your love, and your breath.

1, 2, 3 . . . Ph-e-w-w-w-w-w!
The Universe

Just kidding, I'd never blow you out.

There are only two types of dreams.
Those that have come true. And those that are coming true.

You slay me,
The Universe

Yeah, better start narrowing down the trim choices for your new hovercraft and getting really clear on how many friends you want to take into space.

No matter
how things seem, hope is near and love is present.

In the house,
The Universe

Always.

Can you imagine

an astral plane somewhere "out there" where very old souls could
rendezvous to practice and perfect their most highly developed
manifestation techniques?

A members-only kind of place, where whatever they think about
comes to life in the most vivid, high-definition, surround sound
Technicolor, vis-à-vis the most intricate plots and circumstances?

Where the only limits that exist lie in one's ability to imagine
what they have never before imagined, and to move with it in
anticipation of its "physical" expression?

And best of all, being astral, no harm can come to them. They're completely untouchable. Nothing is real, yet everything matters. And there can be infinite gains in terms of insight and fun, yet no losses since everything is illusory.

Actually, the worst thing that can happen is that they temporarily become so entranced by their creations, they completely forget who they are, where they are, and how powerful they really are.

Yep, it would be exactly like this astral plane.

Only here, to help wake 'em up from their trance, we're experimenting with Notes from the Universe . . .

The easiest way
to make the biggest difference in the world begins with
reaching out, right away, to those nearest.

And they happen to be ready.

As are you.

Yeee-ha!
The Universe

Poised for greatness, you so are.
Lucky people of the world.

The reason your thoughts become things,
besides your insistence, was so that you could always change
whatever you didn't like.

"No exceptions, full on, without judgment, all things possible,
as soon as possible, sky's the limit, where they have chocolate,
please, now, thank you . . ." you were quoted.

Nice word-train,
The Universe

You should have asked for unicorns, too.

Just an FYI:

you're living a temporary life in a temporary world, where
nothing makes you less, everything makes you more, and
no one is truly "done" until everyone is done.

Watch your brothers and sisters,
The Universe

This is how we prepare you for eternity.

Performing miracles

isn't a matter of doing the impossible, it's a matter
of redefining the possible.

Tallyho,
The Universe

Consider, people once thought double chocolate was impossible.

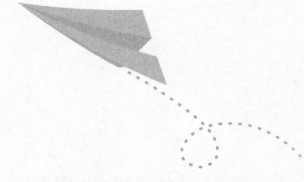

Some people smile to make friends.

Others smile to look younger and live longer.

And then there are those who so totally get life,
that smiling is all they know.

Cheese,
The Universe

*Plus, feeling grateful puts everyone on the fast track
to more of everything wonderful.*

Only in hindsight,

will the miracles become obvious, will you see you were guided,
and will you find there was order all along.

"Otherwise," as you once said, a long, long time ago,
"it would all be too easy . . ."

We agreed,
The Universe

*By the way, we've patented the whole life-self-discovery-thing-in-time-and-space on your behalf, and the royalties have been utterly divine.
Not quite sure how to thank you.*

If you don't

really need to correct someone or something, I say don't.

Especially someone.

Hipsters,
The Universe

Love seeing you love.

When you finally

see what this whole time-space-thing is all about,
you're going to laugh; you're going to cry; and you're going to be
so, so, so, so, so happy you *loved* as much as you did.

Dotingly,
The Universe

What a lover you turned out to be.

Sometimes...

when circumstances or disappointments bump you off track,
it's the beginning of an even bigger dream coming true,
that could not have come true on the track you were on.

Yeah, always.

Always, always—
The Universe

I know what I'm doing and I love you so much.

I gotta confess,

every now and then I get this incredible urge to
splurge on myself. To really indulge. Pull out all the stops.
And tickle every one of my senses.

Yep, and that's when I'll choose a lifetime like yours. With
obstacles to challenge me, people to "test" me, and circumstances
that force me to see things that even I have never seen before.

And a personality like yours, which possesses faith so daring that
even when lost, you still hope. Dreams so bold that even when
you fall, you get back up. And a heart so big that even when
it breaks, as all big hearts do, there's always room for second
chances and new romances.

That's what I do.

Talk about crazy, sexy, and cool!
The Universe

Thanks.

Everyone's lucky, dear.
Few are prepared.

Visualize,
The Universe

Which is kind of like being dealt a royal straight flush and playing "Go Fish."

Actually . . .
dreams come from a future dimension where they already exist,
and the dreamers of such dreams have future selves who now live
there and are oh-so-anxious to show you what is truly possible.

{Sound of crackling, rolling, happy thunder on
a clear and sunny day}
The Universe

Actually, all thunder is happy.

Do you think if someone deeply believed

that they and I were one—that I stirred in their heart, ran through
their veins, and shone from their eyes—they'd wait for the
part of me that existed "outside" of themselves to
make their dreams come true?

Or would they seize each moment of every day,
assured of their inevitable success?

Phew,
The Universe

I work through you, not for you.

Hubba, Hubba, Hubba!
Ya know how the bud of a flower looks?

Already attractive, special, and unique yet still barely hinting
at the splendor and magnificence to come. Oblivious itself
of how its presence will add to the world.

That's what you remind me of.

The Universe

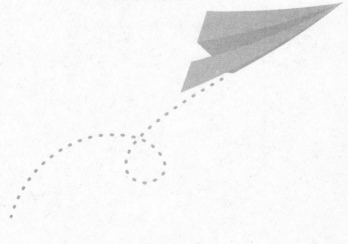

The main reason

someone moves mountains, wins friends, influences people,
amasses a fortune, or anything else, is because they
thought they would.

You can do this,
The Universe

Shall we "Veni, Vidi, Vici!?"

There's nothing

so important that it can't be said tomorrow.

You know . . . if you aren't sure.

Cool jets,
The Universe

ACKNOWLEDGMENTS

I've been extraordinarily blessed by the women in my life—beginning with those in my family and then beyond, into my working and writing life. Without them, I would not be who I am today, nor be able to write, live, and love as fully as I do now. I'd like to express my admiration for one of those women here who for the past fifteen years (of my twenty in-print) has been my sounding board, adviser, and dear friend—Hope Koppelman.

Her work titles have varied from assistant to editor to creative director, but no title could ever capture the importance of her unwavering support and faithful camaraderie. From behind the scenes, she's also given me hope when I was discouraged, brought clarity when I was confused, and enthusiastically celebrated my accomplishments.

Hope, you are a treasure in my life beyond value. "Thank you" seems not enough.

Also by Mike Dooley

Books

An Adventurer's Guide to the Jungles of Time and Space (formerly titled *Lost in Space*)

A Beginner's Guide to the Universe: Uncommon Ideas for Living an Unusually Happy Life

Channeled Lessons from Deep Space (with Tracy Farquhar)

Choose Them Wisely: Thoughts Become Things!

Even More Notes from the Universe: Dancing Life's Dance

Leveraging the Universe: 7 Steps to Engaging Life's Magic

Life on Earth: Understanding Who We Are, How We Got Here, and What May Lie Ahead

Manifesting Change: It Couldn't Be Easier

More Notes from the Universe: Life, Dreams and Happiness

Notes from the Universe: New Perspectives from an Old Friend

Notes from the Universe Coloring Book: Enjoy the Journey

Playing the Matrix: A Program for Living Deliberately and Creating Consciously

The Top 10 Things Dead People Want to Tell YOU

Totally Unique Thoughts: Reminders of Life's Everyday Magic

Card Decks

Notes from the Universe

Notes from the Universe on Abundance

Notes from the Universe on Love & Connection

DVDs

Manifesting Change: It Couldn't Be Easier

The Path Less Traveled: Performing Miracles

Thoughts Become Things

Video Courses

The 21-Day Visualization Project (with Hope Koppelman)

Love Your Life in 30 Days (with Hope Koppelman)

Playing the Matrix: A Laser Focused Series

Playing the Matrix and Getting What You Really Want

A Trainer's Guide to Infinite Possibilities: Certification

For Children

Dreams Come True: All They Need Is You

Your Magical Life

MICHAEL CAIRNS

MIKE DOOLEY is a *New York Times* bestselling author who has presented to live audiences in 156 cities, 42 countries, on 6 continents. Best known as a metaphysical teacher and creator of the Notes from the Universe, his acclaimed books, including *The Top Ten Things Dead People Want to Tell YOU*, *A Beginner's Guide to the Universe*, and *Infinite Possibilities*, have been published worldwide in 27 languages. He's also the founder of TUT's philosophical Adventurers Club, home to over 800,000 online members.